CASEBOOK ON
WAITING FOR GODOT

CASEBOOK ON WAITING FOR GODOT

Edited by Ruby Cohn

GROVE PRESS, INC.
NEW YORK

CONTENTS

INTRODUCTION

Translated into over a dozen languages, *Waiting for Godot* has been performed in little theaters and large theaters, by amateurs and professionals, on radio and television. Less than two decades after the play was written, *Waiting for Godot* has sold nearly 50,000 copies in the original French, and nearly 350,000 copies in Beckett's own English translation. "Extraordinary how mathematics help you to know yourself," as Beckett's Molloy remarked. And mathematics do help you to know the best-seller, the smash hit, but only the individual can know a classic which is a work that provides continuous growth for the individual. Paradoxically for our time, *Waiting for Godot* is a classic that sells well.

The play's action simultaneously affirms and denies its opening line, its closing stage direction. "Nothing to be done." suggests futility in this play of assiduous busyness; *"They do not move."* suggests fixity in this play that moves intensely. And between them, these two problematical negatives contain our civilization, a tragicomedy at evening.

An immense erudition stutters through Lucky's monologue; an immense range of emotion undercuts Pozzo's posturing. Pozzo and Lucky come and go, while Didi and Gogo wait. Grounded on the wooden board, companions of a wooden tree, the two friends wait—their way of knocking on wood. In his four characters, Beckett summarizes human relationships; in their activities, he sums up human living. The two friends, neither servants nor served, are free to fill Godot-less time with prodigious variety—recollection and prediction, mastication and defecation, feeling and playing. Their inexhaustible immediacy forms Beckett's text, while the subtext implies hesitantly, "I act, therefore I am." And even more hesitantly, "I wait, therefore I am—maybe." Acting while waiting, Beckett's characters grasp us all.

After the curtain falls or the book is closed, our own waiting may erupt into dialogue about Samuel Beckett's *Waiting for Godot*. This volume reflects such dialogue.

—RUBY COHN

IMPACT

The First Review

AT THE THÉÂTRE DE BABYLONE: *WAITING FOR GODOT* BY SAMUEL BECKETT

SYLVAIN ZEGEL

Theater-lovers rarely have the pleasure of discovering a new author worthy of the name; an author who can give his dialogue true poetic force, who can animate his characters so vividly that the audience identifies with them, suffering and laughing with them; who, having meditated, does not amuse himself with mere word-juggling; who deserves comparison with the greatest. When this occurs, it is an event which will be spoken of for a long time, and will be remembered years later. In my opinion, Samuel Beckett's first play *Waiting for Godot*, at the Théâtre de Babylone, will be spoken of for a long time.

Perhaps a few grumblers complained that it is "a play in which nothing happens," because they didn't find the more or less conventional plot used by innumerable authors from Aristophanes and Plautus on; or because, on leaving the theater, they couldn't summarize the play, or explain why they had laughed with embarrassed laughter.

They heard people using everyday words, and they did not feel that by an inexplicable miracle—which is called art—the words suddenly acquired a new value. They saw people being happy and suffering, and they did not understand that they were watching their own lives. But when the curtain fell, and they heard the enthusiasm of the audience, they understood at

From *La Libération*, January 7, 1953, reprinted by permission of the author. Translated from the French by Ruby Cohn.

least this much: Paris had just recognized in Samuel Beckett one of today's best playwrights.

It is hard not to be amazed that this is the first play of a writer who has achieved critical acclaim for his novels *Molloy* and *Malone Dies,* since he has mastered all the exigencies of the stage. Each word acts as the author wishes, touching us or making us laugh.

These two tramps, who represent all humanity, utter remarks that any one of us might utter. These two men are feeble and energetic, cowardly and courageous; they bicker, amuse themselves, are bored, speak to each other without understanding. They do all this to keep busy. To pass time. To live or to give themselves the illusion that they are living. They are certain of only one thing: they are waiting for Godot. Who is Godot? They don't know. And in any case, this myth hasn't the same form, the same qualities, for each of them. It might be happiness, eternal life, the ideal and unattainable quest of all men —which they wait for and which gives them the strength to live on. . . .

Fellow Writers

GODOT OR THE MUSIC-HALL SKETCH OF PASCAL'S PENSÉES AS PLAYED BY THE FRATELLINI CLOWNS

JEAN ANOUILH

"Nothing happens, nobody comes, nobody goes, it's awful." This line, spoken by one of the characters in the play, provides its best summary. *Godot* is a masterpiece that will cause despair

From *Arts* #400, January 27, 1953, reprinted by permission of the author. Translated from the French by Ruby Cohn.

for men in general and for playwrights in particular. I think that the opening night at the Théâtre de Babylone is as important as the opening of Pirandello in Paris in 1923, presented by Pitoeff.

One can only raise one's hat—a bowler to be sure, as in the play—and pray to heaven for a little talent. The greatness, the artful playing, a style—we are "somewhere" in the theater. The music-hall sketch of Pascal's *Pensées* as played by the Fratellini clowns.

AT THE BABYLONE
A FORTUNATE MOVE
ON THE THEATER CHECKERBOARD

JACQUES AUDIBERTI

. . . Prophets without prosody, translators without a word-scale in their heads, all those who believe themselves to be writers because they have written that they are—I invite all of these to listen to Samuel Beckett's *Waiting for Godot* at the Théâtre de Babylone, a perfect work which deserves a triumph.

I won't narrate the play for you; does one narrate a landscape, a face, a pattern, an emotion? One can describe them, or interpret them.

Two tramps wait for Godot on a road, in the company of a tree that is too delicate to be used for hanging oneself. Tired and hungry though they are, they talk continuously. Their sentences are broken. What are they doing? Waiting. For whom? Godot.

They speak like Charlie Chaplin. As he would have spoken,

From *Arts* #394, January 16, 1953, reprinted by permission of Mme. Ponty-Audiberti. Translated from the French by Ruby Cohn.

not as the Count of Limelahight, but when he had nothing to say. But this play does not need references or relationships.

Godot doesn't come. At least not this evening. But they are there every evening to wait for him. Nothing comes, except the moon, and a delirious fake blind man in a greatcoat—Pozzo. On a leash, he keeps a domesticated skeleton who knows how to think. To think inexhaustibly, aloud, on command. Nothing comes, except a child who says nothing but that Godot will not come. Probably Godot will never come.

Now then, perhaps Godot has come; it might be Pozzo. Not heartening, if the man in the greatcoat should be God. What! God? Again!

Please note that the author doesn't say so, but he forces us to say it. In "Godot" there is "God." Besides, the waiting men give to this Godot whom they have never seen the white beard and the old age of portraits of the Eternal. But Godot might just as well be a neighboring farmer who could give work to the tramps, and Pozzo might be a raving squire. Symbolism is optional, but applause is obligatory. . . .

IT IS NOT AN ACCIDENT
BUT A TRIUMPH

ARMAND SALACROU

An unexpected play which we nevertheless recognize; we were waiting for this play of our time, with its new tone, its simple and modest language, and its closed circular plot from which no exit is possible. This new and yet instantly familiar dialogue forms part of our lives within a few hours, and then stays with

From *Arts* #400, January 27, 1953, reprinted by permission of the author. Translated from the French by Ruby Cohn.

us. This play is not unique; we have already heard Adamov, Shéhadé, Meckert, Boris Vian, Pichette, Jean Vauthier, Ionesco. But this time there is co-operation on the part of the public, who participate in the play; it is a triumph. Why throw the name of Kafka into this setting and these characters, like a ball into ninepins? That which comes from nothing, goes nowhere.

I was told that at the end of the performance, a well-known playwright remarked to his director: "And to think that I torture my brain to invent plot. But this fellow hasn't scratched the surface of his gray matter." That is precisely the incomparable contribution of Samuel Beckett. He has made no attempt to modify the 36 (or 200,000, depending on one's authority) basic dramatic plots. No. With clear gestures and obvious words, he simply tells us a story that isn't one. . . , and this story with neither beginning nor end captivates us because it is our story. *Waiting for Godot* is not an accident. An author has appeared, who has taken us by the hand to lead us into his universe.

SAMUEL BECKETT
OR PRESENCE ON THE STAGE

ALAIN ROBBE-GRILLET

[*Waiting for Godot*] *holds together*, without a hollow, though it consists of nothing but emptiness, without a break, though it would seem to have no reason to continue or to conclude. From beginning to end, the audience follows; it may

---

From *For a New Novel* (New York: Grove Press, Inc., 1965), copyright © 1965 by Grove Press, Inc., translated by Richard Howard. Reprinted by permission. The article originally appeared in *Critique*, February, 1953, and has since been revised by the author.

lose countenance sometimes, but remains somehow compelled by these two beings, who do nothing, who say virtually nothing, who have no other quality than to be present.

From the very first performance, the virtually unanimous critics have emphasized the *public* character of the spectacle. As a matter of fact, the words "experimental theater" no longer apply here: what we have is simply theater, which everyone can see, from which everyone immediately derives his enjoyment.

Is this to say that no one misjudges it? Of course not. *Godot* is misjudged in every way, just as everyone misjudges his own misery. There is no lack of explanations, which are offered from every side, left and right, each more futile than the next:

Godot is God. Don't you see that the word is the diminutive of the root-word *God* which the author has borrowed from his mother tongue? After all, why not? Godot—why not, just as well?—is the earthly ideal of a better social order. Do we not aspire to a better life, better food, better clothes, as well as to the possibility of no longer being beaten? And this Pozzo, who is precisely *not* Godot—is he not the man who keeps thought enslaved? Or else Godot is death: tomorrow we will hang ourselves, if it does not come all by itself. Godot is silence; we must speak *while waiting for it*: in order to have the right, ultimately, to keep still. Godot is that inaccessible *self* Beckett pursues through his entire *œuvre*, with this constant hope: "This time, perhaps, it will be me, at last."

But these images, even the most ridiculous ones, which thus try as best they can to limit the damages, do not obliterate from anyone's mind the reality of the drama itself, that part which is both the most profound and quite superficial, about which there is nothing else to say: Godot is that character for whom two tramps are waiting at the edge of a road, and who does not come.

As for Gogo and Didi, they refuse even more stubbornly any other signification than the most banal, the most immediate one: they are men. And their situation is summed up in this simple observation, beyond which it does not seem possible to advance: they are *there*, they are on the stage.

Attempts doubtless already existed, for some time, which rejected the stage movement of the bourgeois theater. *Godot,*
however, marks in this realm a kind of finality. Nowhere had
the risk been so great, for what is involved this time, without
ambiguity, is what is essential; nowhere, moreover, have the
means employed been so *poor;* yet never, ultimately, has the
margin of misunderstanding been so negligible. To such a degree that we must turn back in order to measure this risk and
this poverty.

It seemed reasonable to suppose, until recent years, that although the novel for example could free itself of many of its
rules and traditional accessories, the theater at least had to show
more discretion. The dramatic work, as a matter of fact, ac-
cedes to its true life only on condition of an understanding
with a public of some kind or other; hence the latter must be
surrounded with attentions: it must be offered unusual characters, it must be interested by piquant situations, it must be
caught up in the complications of a plot, or else it must be
violently taken out of itself by a continuous verbal invention,
deriving more or less from delirium or from poetic lyricism.

What does *Waiting for Godot* offer us? It is hardly enough
to say that nothing happens in it. That there should be neither
complications nor plot of any kind has already been the case
on other stages. Here, it is *less than nothing,* we should say: as
if we were watching a kind of regression *beyond* nothing. As
always in Samuel Beckett, what little had been given to us at
the start—and which seemed to be nothing—is soon corrupted
before our eyes, degraded further, like Pozzo who returns deprived of sight, dragged on by Lucky deprived of speech—and
like, too, that carrot which in the second act is no longer anything but a radish. . . .

"This is becoming really insignificant," one of the vagabonds
says at this point. "Not enough," says the other. And a long
silence punctuates his answer.

It will be evident, from these two lines, what distance we
have come from the verbal delirium mentioned above. From
start to finish, the dialogue of *Godot* is *moribund,* extenuated,

constantly located at those frontiers of agony where all of Beckett's "heroes" move, concerning whom we often cannot even be certain that they are still on this side of their death. In the middle of these silences, these repetitions, these ready-made phrases (typical: "One is what one is. The inside doesn't change."), one tramp or the other proposes, now and then, in order to pass the time, that they make conversation, "repent," hang themselves, tell stories, insult each other, play "Pozzo and Lucky," but each time the attempt breaks down and peters out, after a few uncertain exchanges, into suspension points, renunciations, failures.

As for the argument, it is summarized in four words: "We're waiting for Godot"—which continually recur, like a refrain. But like a stupid and tiresome refrain, for such waiting interests no one; it does not possess, as waiting, the slightest stage value. It is neither a hope, nor an anguish, nor even a despair. It is barely an alibi.

In this general dilapidation, there is a kind of culminating point—that is to say, under the circumstances, the reverse of a culminating point: a nadir, an oubliette. Lucky and Pozzo, feeble now, have collapsed on top of each other in the middle of the road; they cannot get back up. After a long argument, Didi comes to their aid, but he stumbles and falls on top of *them*; he must call for help in his turn. Gogo holds out his hand, loses his balance, and falls. There is no longer a single character standing up. There is nothing left on stage but this wriggling, whining heap, in which we then observe Didi's face light up as he says, in a voice almost calm again, "We are men!"

We all know what the "theater of ideas" was: a healthy exercise of the intelligence, which had its public (though it sometimes treated situations and dramatic development in a rather cavalier way). We were somewhat bored in this theater, but we "thought" hard there, out front as well as on stage. Thought, even subversive thought, always has something reassuring about it. Speech—beautiful language—is reassuring too. How many misunderstandings a noble and harmonious discourse has created, serving as a mask either for ideas or for their absence!

Here, no misunderstanding: in *Godot* there is no more thought than there is beautiful language; neither one nor the other figures in the text except in the form of parody, of *inside out* once again, or of corpse.

Language is that "twilight" described by Pozzo; announced as a setpiece by a great deal of throat-clearing and whip-cracking, crammed with sounding phrases and dramatic gestures, but sabotaged at the same time by sudden interruptions, familiar exclamations, grotesque lapses in inspiration. . . .

And then comes the thought. The two tramps have asked Pozzo a question, but no one can recall what it was. All three simultaneously take off their hats, raise their hands to their foreheads, concentrate intensely. Long silence. Suddenly Gogo makes an exclamation, he has remembered: "Why doesn't he put down his bags?"

He is referring to Lucky. This is, as a matter of fact, the question which had been asked some moments before, but in the interval the servant has put down the bags; hence Didi convinces everyone by concluding: "Since he has put down his bags it is impossible we should have asked why he does not do so." [p. 27b]* Which is logic itself. In this universe where time does not pass, the words *before* and *after* have no meaning; only the present situation counts: the bags *are* down, as if forever.

Such reasoning was already to be found in Lewis Carroll or in Jarry. Beckett does better: he gives us a specialized thinker, Lucky. . . . In order to shut him up, the others are forced to knock him over, beat him up, trample on him, and—the only really effective method—to take off his hat. As one of the two vagabonds says: "Thinking isn't the worst."

We cannot overemphasize the seriousness of such reflections. Over seventy centuries of analysis and metaphysics have a tendency, instead of making us modest, to conceal from us the

---

* All page references, except when otherwise indicated, are to the American edition of *Waiting for Godot* (New York: Grove Press, Inc., 1954).

weakness of our resources when it comes to essentials. As a matter of fact, everything happens as if the real importance of a question was measured, precisely, by our incapacity to apply honest thinking to it, unless to make it retrogress.

It is this movement—this dangerously contagious retrogression—which all of Beckett's work suggests. The two confederates, Pozzo and Lucky, have thus declined from one act to the other, in the fashion of Murphy, Molloy, Malone, etc. The carrots have been reduced to radishes. As for the cyclical song of the thieving dog, Didi has even ended by losing the thread of it. And this is in keeping with all the other accessories of the play.

But the two tramps remain intact, unchanged. Hence we are certain, this time, that they are not mere marionettes whose role is confined to concealing the absence of the protagonist. It is not this Godot they are supposed to be waiting for *who has* "*to be*," but they, Didi and Gogo.

We grasp at once, as we watch them, this major function of theatrical representation: to show of what the fact of *being there* consists. For it is this, precisely, which we had not yet seen on a stage, or in any case which we had not seen so clearly, with so few concessions. The dramatic character, in most cases, merely *plays a role*, like the people around us who evade their own existence. In Beckett's play, on the contrary, everything happens as if the two tramps were on stage *without having a role*.

They *are there*; they must explain themselves. But they do not seem to have a text prepared beforehand and scrupulously learned by heart, to support them. They must invent. They are free.

Of course, this freedom is without any use: just as they have nothing to recite, they have nothing to *invent* either; and their conversation, which no plot sustains, is reduced to ridiculous fragments: stock responses, puns, more or less abortive phony arguments. They try a little bit of everything, at random. The only thing they are not free to do is to leave, to cease *being there*: they must remain because they are waiting for Godot.

They are there in the first act, from the beginning to the end, and when the curtain falls it does so, despite the announcement of their departure, on two men who continue waiting. They are still there in the second act, which brings nothing new; and again, despite the announcement of their departure, they remain on stage when the curtain falls. They will still be there the next day, the day after that, and so on . . . *tomorrow and tomorrow and tomorrow . . . from day to day* . . . alone on stage, standing there, futile, without past or future, irremediably present.

The First Director

ROGER BLIN AT WORK

JOHN FLETCHER

Beckett's French director and close friend, Roger Blin, was in Toulouse, in southern France, not long ago, spending about a month with a local company rehearsing *En attendant Godot*. The company, Le Grenier de Toulouse, was first founded in March, 1945, by the dynamic Maurice Sarrazin. Since the play is not an easy one, it was natural for them to ask Roger Blin down from Paris to produce it for them.

This is the fourth or fifth time he has staged it. He has even directed German actors in the German translation, although he speaks little or no German himself; he worked through an interpreter. Each time he approaches the text afresh, because although he has his own idea of how the play should be performed (an idea worked out in close collaboration with the

From *Modern Drama*, February, 1966, reprinted by permission and modified by the author.

author), he must inevitably adjust that idea in accordance with differing circumstances and different personalities of his actors. This time, for instance, he had as Pozzo a bulky, slow actor in his sixties, with booming voice and silvery hair and a tendency to grunt and gurgle in his throat, Jean Hort—the ideal man for the part, as Blin admitted, saying that Hort would be the best Pozzo the French stage had seen. Blin himself played Pozzo in the original Théâtre de Babylone production in 1953, but he says he was never happy in the role, because being tall and thin he had not the physique it requires, and thus not the right stage presence. Blin's person is impressive: tall, gangling even, very nervous, full of tics and facial twitches, stuttering when he speaks, blinking all the time and often rubbing his eyes, but transformed the moment he acts, in order to demonstrate a movement, in order to speak a line. Then, at once, all the twitching and stuttering goes, his deep, melodious voice breaks out clear and unhurried, his body under complete control. The differences between Blin off-stage and Blin on-stage could not be more striking. He is another man altogether.

His manner of directing actors is strangely detached. He stands watching them sometimes, moving little, infrequently smoking short black cigars. More often he sits slumped in a chair, with his legs interwoven, his hands dangling, his eyes closed. He intervenes rarely, and when he does, it is only after a preliminary stutter. When he has to interrupt, he prefers to go on stage and demonstrate the actions, speak the words himself. One sees him now burping happily on his stool as Pozzo, now waddling painfully as Vladimir, now shaking with Lucky's palsy. "You need to be very fit to play Beckett's decrepits," he says, and seeing Bousquet (Vladimir) sweating profusely toward the end of a rehearsal one agrees with him. Each time that he demonstrates something, his authority is undeniable; and one sees his familiar production coming to life before one's eyes. Blin has this play in the palm of his hand; he reveals new facets in it every moment one watches him at work on it. As he teaches Granville to shake and puff and pant like Lucky, a question occurs to me. How did Jean Martin, the original Lucky, come by that frightening but unforgettable ague? He thought it up himself, it seems, and adopted it from the start, and neither author nor producer felt any need to ask him to modify it; the only trouble was that it affected him deeply, and he took months to lose the fidgets which prevented him taking other parts after the end of *Godot's* run. Blin shows Granville how to do it, without of course insisting on an exact imitation; he respects each actor's characteristics. In particular, Granville has not Martin's high-pitched voice verging on the scream, and so Blin lets him say the words in his normal pitch of voice.

As rehearsals progress, Blin tightens things up, but always gradually, with elaborate politeness; always slightly withdrawn, he never orders, only requests, and is never familiar. He is evidently too shy to impose himself or to become "chummy." Rehearsals last all afternoon and recommence after a break for dinner; they then go on till midnight. For practical reasons of availability of stage room, the afternoons are given over to working mainly on the text and on enunciation in an empty cinema, with the actors either on the narrow stage or reclining in the red plush seats. In the evening, in a large barnlike hall with a big stage at one end and Grenier posters everywhere, actors and producer get down to the concrete details of the movements. As the days pass, the initial hesitations are resolved, the untidinesses ironed out. The actors have learned their words and their movements; even the complicated clown-games demanded of Vladimir and Estragon are becoming more automatic. The play starts to exert its power. Hort has fully mastered his role, and true to the author's direction is "suddenly furious" when, in Act II, he rails at the two men for "tormenting me with your accursed time"—and then his fury drops, his voice takes on the accents of poetry as he speaks the now famous words, "they give birth astride of a grave . . ." [p. 57b] The play, with all its drama and its farce, its pathos and its humor, is ready to take to the road, and Blin's role is nearly finished. In his free mornings, and even in odd moments during rehearsals, he is (unlike the author) ready to talk about his work.

He speaks of his past, of the effect Surrealism had on him, and of his friendship with Antonin Artaud. The extraordinarily fortunate meeting with Beckett was not a result of pure chance. In 1949, at the Gaîté-Montparnasse theater, Blin was putting on Strindberg's *Ghost Sonata* when Beckett came to see it. He came again, and thinking that Blin was the man to put on the play (*En attendant Godot*) that he had recently written, sent him a copy of the typescript. It was not until some time later that Blin actually made Beckett's acquaintance; far too shy to face Blin himself, Beckett dealt at first through his wife Suzanne. When they did finally meet, Blin was curious to know why Beckett had chosen him. Because Blin was faithful to Strindberg, both to the letter and to the spirit, and because the theater was nearly empty, was the answer. Beckett was sure that Blin would therefore respect his own text and insure that the place be empty, which seemed to the author the ideal condition for a good performance.

Not deterred by the eccentricity of this view, Blin was won over by the play. He says that at first he did not see the full import of its theme, but was impressed by the quality of the dialogue and characterization. Unable to persuade the Gaîté-Montparnasse to take the play (soon afterward, in any case, the theater went bankrupt), Blin had to wait three years to put it on. A small official bursary enabled him, early in 1953, to stage the play at Serreau's Théâtre de Babylone and bring off a triumph. The choice of *Godot* itself, however, was largely fortuitous. Blin had in his hands at the same time Beckett's first (and still unpublished and unperformed) play, *Eleuthéria,* and decided against it in the end mainly because *Godot* required only five characters, whereas *Eleuthéria* demanded over three times that number, and money was short. The greater maturity and profundity of *Godot* was not at the time a major consideration. Since those days Blin has been responsible for putting on Beckett's plays in France, and *Happy Days,* with Madeleine Renaud, was a recent success. *Play* was staged by Jean-Marie Serreau, but Blin's pupil, Delphine Seyrig, acted in it. As an actor, Blin will probably be best remembered for his masterly interpretation of Hamm in the creation of *Endgame* in 1957, which he also, of course, directed (the play is, incidentally, dedicated to him).

Blin seems to be a little disturbed by the way Beckett is developing theatrically, since he feels that there is less and less scope for the director in the carefully annotated texts Beckett is writing now. One has only to compare the text of *Godot* with that of *Play* to see what Blin means: the minute instructions in the latter would daunt any independent-minded producer. During the first rehearsals of *Godot* Beckett was, it seems, much less sure of himself as a writer of drama and was quite open to suggestion from a professional like Blin. It was at Blin's instigation that he suppressed several passages that seemed too long or literary, or that seemed to break the tension in some way. Thus, all the omissions that critics have noted in the English text, compared with the original French, are those practiced by Blin in production and therefore left out by the author from his English translation (the same applies to a passage omitted from *Endgame*). Beckett also suppressed from his French text, at Blin's suggestion, a reference to Bim and Bom, "the Stalinist comedians"—which can still be seen in the first French edition of 1952 [p. 56] but not in subsequent editions. One of Vladimir's replies, too, is much longer in the first edition [p. 99], but Blin shortened it for being too "literary" and pretentious; on the other hand, Blin occasionally adds, for instance another *"voyons"* from Vladimir [p. 109] since the situation seems to require it. But Beckett modified his text himself sometimes: a forceful *"debout!"* ("Up, pig!") is added to Pozzo's words (preliminary to his departure in Act II) between the first and subsequent editions. And Beckett himself thought of the improvement recorded in later editions, *"ce n'est pas le vide qui manque"* ("there's no lack of void"), instead of *"ce n'est pas l'espace qui manque"* ("there's no lack of space"); on the other hand, Blin drew Beckett's attention to an Anglicism in the typescript, *"l'une de trois choses"* ("one of three things"), corrected in the published text to *"de deux choses l'une"* ("one of two things"). Moreover, Beckett does not specify in the French text the insults Estragon and Vladimir are required to exchange in the middle of Act II; when he and Blin discussed it, they decided to employ several common terms of abuse, and to end up with "Architect!" Blin had heard one Belgian taxi-driver use it to another, and afterward learnt what it meant. A quarter of Brussels had been scheduled for demolition by the city's architect, it appears, and for the dispossessed inhabitants the worst and cruellest gibe imaginable was therefore "Architect!" and soon others adopted it, too. It is certainly forceful and effective in Blin's production. As for the name "Godot" which has caused so much controversy, Blin says Beckett told him that it was suggested quite simply by the words for boot in popular French, *godillot, godasse,* because of the prominent role footwear enjoys in the play. Vladimir's song at the beginning of Act II, "A dog came in the kitchen, And stole a crust of bread," is, according to Blin, a German student round song, translated by Beckett but with its original tune preserved: *"Ein Hund kam in die Küche . . ."*

Blin had several things to say about the author of the play. The cruelty in his work was, he maintained, a form of self-defense against an acute sensibility, and he told how, once going through the quarter of Les Halles in Paris with Beckett, he noticed how the latter started on seeing animal heads and offal in a cart, and how much the sight of blood affected him. The same thing can no doubt be said to apply to the violently obscene parts of Beckett's work; the idea of cruelty and obscenity as a reaction of defense in his writings is worth serious investigation.

An English Review

TOMORROW

HAROLD HOBSON

The objections to Mr. Samuel Beckett's play as a theatrical entertainment are many and obvious. Anyone keen-sighted enough to see a church at noonday can perceive what they are. *Waiting for Godot* has nothing at all to seduce the senses. Its drab, bare scene is dominated by a withered tree and a garbage can, and for a large part of the evening this lugubrious setting, which makes the worst of both town and country, is inhabited only by a couple of tramps, verminous, decayed, their hats broken and their clothes soiled, with sweaty feet, inconstant bladders, and boils on the backside.

This is not all. In the course of the play, nothing happens. Such dramatic progress as there is, is not toward a climax, but toward a perpetual postponement. Vladimir and Estragon are waiting for Godot, but this gentleman's appearance (*if* he is a gentleman, and not something of another species) is not prepared with any recognizable theatrical tension, for the audience knows well enough from the beginning that Godot will never come. The dialogue is studded with words that have no meaning for normal ears; repeatedly the play announces that it has come to a stop, and will have to start again; never does it reconcile itself with reason.

It is hardly surprising that, English audiences notoriously disliking anything not immediately understandable, certain early lines in the play, such as, "I have had better entertainment elsewhere," were received on the first night with ironical laughter;

From *The Sunday Times* (London), August 7, 1955, reprinted by permission.

or that when one of the characters yawned, the yawn was echoed and amplified by a humorist in the stalls. Yet at the end the play was warmly applauded. There were even a few calls for "Author!" But these were rather shamefaced cries, as if those who uttered them doubted whether it were seemly to make too much noise whilst turning their coats.

Strange as the play is, and curious as are its processes or thought, it has a meaning; and this meaning is untrue. To attempt to put this meaning into a paragraph is like trying to catch Leviathan in a butterfly net, but nevertheless the effort must be made. The upshot of *Waiting for Godot* is that the two tramps are always waiting for the future, their ruinous consolation being that there is always tomorrow; they never realize that today is today. In this, says Mr. Beckett, they are like humanity, which dawdles and drivels away its life, postponing action, eschewing enjoyment, waiting only for some far-off, divine event, the millennium, the Day of Judgment.

Mr. Beckett has, of course, got it all wrong. Humanity worries very little over the Day of Judgment. It is far too busy hire-purchasing television sets, popping into three-star restaurants, planting itself vineyards, building helicopters. But he has got it wrong in a tremendous way. And this is what matters. There is no need at all for a dramatist to philosophize rightly: he can leave that to the philosophers. But it is essential that if he philosophizes wrongly, he should do so with swagger. Mr. Beckett has any amount of swagger. A dusty, coarse, irreverent, pessimistic, violent swagger? Possibly. But the genuine thing, the real McCoy.

Vladimir and Estragon have each a kind of universality. They wear their rags with a difference. Vladimir is eternally hopeful; if Godot does not come this evening, then he will certainly arrive tomorrow, or at the very latest the day after. Estragon, much troubled by his boots, is less confident. He thinks the game is not worth playing, and is ready to hang himself. Or so he says. But he does nothing. Like Vladimir, he only talks. They both idly spin away the great top of their life in the vain expectation that some master whip will one day give it eternal vitality. Meanwhile their conversation often has the simplicity, in this case the delusive simplicity, of music-hall cross talk, now and again pierced with a shaft that seems for a second or so to touch the edge of truth's garment. It is bewildering. It is exasperating. It is insidiously exciting.

Then there is Pozzo, the big, brutal bully, and the terrible, white-faced gibbering slave he leads about on the end of a rope. These are exasperating, too, but they have astonishing moments of theatrical effectiveness. The long speech into which the silent Lucky breaks, crammed with the unintelligible, with vain repetitions, with the lumber of ill-assorted learning, the pitiful heritage of the ages, the fruits of civilization squashed down and rotten, is horrifyingly delivered by Mr. Timothy Bateson.

Equally startling and impressive is Mr. Peter Bull's sudden expression of Pozzo's anguish, when he cries out that one is born, and one eats, and then one dies, and that is all. This Bull's bellow, if I may call it so, troubles the memory like the swan song of humanity. Mr. Paul Daneman and Mr. Peter Woodthorpe play the tramps without faltering, and the last scene, in which a little boy is involved, has a haunting and inexplicable beauty. Over the whole play lies a great and sad compassion.

Go and see *Waiting for Godot*. At the worst you will discover a curiosity, a four-leaved clover, a black tulip; at the best something that will securely lodge in a corner of your mind for as long as you live.

An American Reaction

TWO TRAMPS

MARYA MANNES

Two talented and emotional representatives of the creative life pressed me to see *Waiting for Godot,* assuring me that this was the one bright spot in the intellectual desert of England. It is the work of Samuel Beckett, who used to be secretary to James Joyce, and who prefers to write in French. The play was produced first in Paris, then translated and produced at the experimental Arts Theatre in London, where it was greeted with such transports that it finally made the West End this summer. "*Godot* is a wonderfully, wonderfully successful, tremendously funny, deeply sad, and exquisite piece of theatrical contrivance and lovingly, yes lovingly, done," caroled Jack Lambert, a BBC critic. "I shan't be surprised if the play does produce a minor theatrical revolution," added another, Paul Delm.

I saw it at a matinee with the house half empty, and I doubt whether I have seen a worse play. I mention it only as typical of the self-delusion of which certain intellectuals are capable, embracing obscurity, pretense, ugliness, and negation as protective coloring for their own confusions.

The play concerns two tramps who inform each other and the audience at the outset that they smell. It takes place in what appears to be the town dump, with a blasted tree rising out of a welter of rusting junk, including plumbing parts. They talk gibberish to each other and to two "symbolic" maniacs for several hours, their dialogue punctuated every few minutes by such remarks as "What are we waiting for?", "Nothing is happening," and "Let us hang ourselves." The last was a good suggestion, unhappily discarded.

No, I don't think stratification has set in among Broadway playgoers. After all, everybody recommends a hit. Everybody, that is, except that very special group, so proudly divorced from all others, that would wait for *Godot* here too, dump and all.

An Irish Evaluation

WAITING WITH BECKETT

DENIS JOHNSTON

Waiting for Godot is a play by Samuel Beckett, late of Dublin, written originally in French, and now translated back into his native idiom by the author himself, obstructed (so far as the English edition is concerned) by some attentions from Her Majesty's Lord Chamberlain. It is about two tramps who are waiting in no particular place for somebody called Godot.

A celebrated cartoon in an American magazine depicted two middle western ladies at a performance of *The Fire Bird* in Monte Carlo. Observing the prima ballerina in one of her more intricate *fouettés*, one lady turns to the other and remarks, "Doesn't she remind you a little of Mrs. Weintraub?"

In much the same spirit, whenever anything out of the ordinary appears hereabouts in print or on the stage, there is always some character who may be relied on to observe that it is influenced by our own local boy, Joyce. And as Joyce is an echoing cistern where every influence from Dante to Amanda Ros can be heard, it is as easy to prove that any experimental writer must be his disciple as it is to show that all the words he employs are also to be found in Webster's dictionary.

From *Irish Writing*, Spring, 1956, reprinted by kind permission of the author and of Sean J. White.

This nuisance is particularly rampant in the case of Sam Beckett, who was, of course, Joyce's powder monkey for some years, and attended the obsequies known as Finnegans Wake. Yet Joyce never had either the economy or the discipline to write a respectable play. Nor was he a thinker, as Beckett clearly is. It is true, of course, that *Waiting for Godot* has in its construction the same spiral, repetitive pattern that was beloved of the Clongownian in his latter years. In general outline, the second part follows the structure of the first—although on a different level—and the audience is led back precisely to the point from which it started. There is talk of boots—of the first Tramp, Estragon, having been beaten by some persons unknown. Were they here yesterday, or were they not? They had better separate (but don't). They had better hang themselves (but don't). Somebody eats a carrot, and then Pozzo arrives with his luckless porter harnessed in a halter. Estragon's feet begin to hurt, which signalizes the approach of a little boy with a message from Mr. Godot. The boy denies that he was there before. The moon comes out, and each scene ends with the line: "Yes, let's go." (But they do not move.)

Yet only a very superficial observer will imagine from this that Beckett is following after Good King Wenceslas. The fact is, that Joyce and he are both pupils of Vico, and merely coincide in their acceptance of Vico's repetitive conception of life. Things that are both equal to this Philosophy of the Barrel Organ must to some extent be equal to one another. But here the resemblance ends, and while Joyce is a master of formlessness, Beckett has a sense of shape that makes each step in his play as inevitable as Anglican Morning Prayer.

He has, however, provided us with a difficult and allusive text for stage purposes which might, at first glance, be as readily the work of a hoaxer as a play of serious importance. The cult of obscurity sits less comfortably in the theater than in the realms of poetry, music, and the fine arts, and Beckett, himself, in some of his previous work has occasionally nourished our suspicions. He has shown himself quite ready to write the prevailing gobbledygook of the Little Reviews. And titles

such as *Whoroscope* and *More Pricks than Kicks* suggest that
he may perhaps have been numbered amongst those who
started their literary careers by scribbling words in the Foxrock
train on the way home from Earlsfort House.

So, when we find the Lord Chamberlain coming to grips
with the problems of flybuttons, tumescence, and urination, we
may feel some legitimate doubts as to the artistic integrity that
insists on their presence. However, the Lord Chamberlain, as
usual, comes out worst in the end by insisting on such inane
changes as the alteration of the Russian name, Fartov, to
Popov, and by inflicting a certain Mrs. Gozzo with warts, in
preference to the clap. A further examination of the cuts and
legitimate amendments that have appeared in the text since
the publication of the original French version, makes it clear
that the author himself has been seriously concerned with the
problem of saying what he means. So, if it matters to him, it is
presumably worth our while as well.

It is also of some interest to note that in translation, both
the American and the English version tend to adopt the vocab-
ulary of the author's native city. *Bavarder* becomes "Blathered,"
and the expression *Ton Bonhomme* assumes the familiar line-
aments of "Your Man"; *alors nous serions baisés* appears as
"Then we'll be banjaxed" (or "ballocksed" for the benefit of
the Americans). And Normandie becomes Connemara. On the
other hand the Tour Eiffel does not become the expected Nel-
son Pillar, and while Voltaire becomes Bishop Berkeley in the
United States, he appears as Doctor Johnson over here—surely
both very peculiar alternatives. Two or three half-page cuts
from the French version, toward the end of the second part,
serve to quicken the climax in English, and show an apprecia-
tion of stage tempo for which we can probably thank the Paris
production.

All these clues may be unimportant if considered separately,
but taken collectively they do indicate a healthy state of affairs
—that the play is a living thing, undergoing the changes and
modifications that all serious drama must undergo in the course
of production, and that the author is fussy about his canon.

From which we may assume that it is not a stunt, and may turn out, on more careful examination, to be far from obscure.

Toward the middle of the last scene, at the point where most dramatists may be assumed to be concerned about what they are getting at, we find this passage:

> What are we doing here, that is the question. And we are blessed in this, that we happen to know the answer. Yes, in this immense confusion one thing alone is clear. We are waiting for Godot to come—[. . .] Or for night to fall. . . . We have kept our appointment, and that's an end to that. We are not saints, but we have kept our appointment. How many people can boast as much?   [p. 51b]

How tempting in the light of this straightforward statement of the play's intention, to jump to the facile conclusion that it is also a parable, and that all we have to do is to fill in an agreed set of proper names, and lo, we have the whole thing on a plate. Godot is God; Pozzo—shall we say—is the Pope; and Vladimir—if you like—is the Duke of Windsor. But, fortunately, Mr. Beckett is much too clever to have fashioned anything that can be solved by means of a crib. An allegory is supposed to be like life, but life is like *Waiting for Godot*, as it is like *Alice in Wonderland*. If it could be easily translated it would cease to have general application. If Mr. Beckett were to admit that Godot is the Almighty, his play would cease to be of such interest to those who do not concur with Lucky in his picture of the great quaquaquaqua. Nor should we be led astray by any similarities in names. The play was originally written in French, in which tongue the name of this maker of missed appointments bears no resemblance to Le Bon Dieu.

In short, Mr. Beckett is no simple arithmetician, and is not attempting to say anything so banal as the fact that two and two make four—or even five. His play is algebraic, in that its characters have the quality of X. And what X means, depends not upon him, but upon us. If you feel that the point of this life—the Intangible for which you may be waiting—is God, then indeed you may accept that solution as your X. If, on the other hand, you feel no such thing, then the play can still have a validity in other terms.

Herein lies the great importance of Mr. Beckett's keeping his trap shut, so far as explanations are concerned, so leaving us free to draw our own conclusions, without any rumbles from the horse's mouth. Sam having written a play of universal application, it might well be argued that any exegesis from him might turn out to be just as wrong as ours. Authors do not always know the best way in which their plays ought to be produced, and the same paradox may apply with equal force to their efforts to explain their significance.

To me, personally, *Waiting for Godot* has an intelligibility which I understand, but do not fully agree with. The two tramps, Estragon and Vladimir, form one composite character— the Observer—the protesting feet, and the head that searches vainly in its hat for something to say next. "It is too much for one man" as somebody remarks. Pozzo and his willing and deeply masochistic slave, Lucky, offer a not unrecognizable picture of my fellow men, comfortably chewing chicken bones until struck blind, slavishly enjoying the halter, and treacherously repaying with a hack on the shins any effort to help them. In particular one should note that superb pastiche of the religious and philosophical ideas of the average Western man that is embodied in Lucky's solitary speech, where the prose hesitates at each hurdle and then goes back to try again, like a horse balking at a jump. It is an especial loss when the words of this speech are thrown away in production by gabbling or inaudibility.

Finally we have the little boy—Mr. Godot's messenger—the ill-paid keeper of the goats, who appears from time to time to tell us that Mr. Godot promises faithfully to arrive tomorrow, although unfortunately unable to come tonight. If this is not the message of the Church, it is hard to see what else it can be. And how despairingly apt is the only possible answer of the race, already quoted: "We have kept our appointment, and that's an end to that."

Meanwhile, Mr. Beckett, who is no quietist, is not content

simply to stand and wait. Vladimir feels that there is something
to be done, even if it is only in helping the blind Pozzo to his
feet.

> Let us do something, while we have the chance! It is not
> every day that we are needed. Not indeed that we personally
> are needed. Others would meet the case equally well, if not
> better. To all mankind they were addressed, those cries for
> help still ringing in our ears! But at this place, at this mo-
> ment of time, all mankind is us, whether we like it or not.
> Let us make the most of it, before it is too late! Let us repre-
> sent worthily for once the foul brood to which a cruel fate
> consigned us!   [p. 51a]

We may not all have experienced so defiant a sense of dedi-
cation as our prophet Samuel exhibits here. We are here, he is
saying, at life's command. If nothing or nobody turns up to
meet us, that at any rate, is not our fault. We have kept our
appointment. And in the meantime we can lend a hand, even
if nobody wants us personally. It is a challenge to Heaven in a
poignant and dignified tone, and in default of its being taken
up, the fact that Mr. Beckett feels that some sort of activity is
of value for its own sake shows that there is more in him of
Sartre than of St. Simeon Stylites.

But although there is no difficulty in abstracting a meaning
from the general impact of the play, there is still plenty left for
writers of theses to mull over in the years to come. What is the
meaning of the names of the characters—except perhaps Lucky,
the only English name in the bunch, and the only apparent
misnomer? And why does the little boy address Vladimir on
each occasion as "Mr. Albert," receiving no correction therein?
Why do Estragon's feet always begin to hurt him, just before
the arrival of this Messenger? And why is the tree the only
living thing that changes for the better? Who are the ten who
beat up Estragon before each curtain rises? And why does this
same enigmatic character give his name to Pozzo as Catullus in

Paris, then change it to Adam in the United States, and finally change it back to Catullus for the benefit of the West End?

While these heavy problems remain unsolved, it is still open to you and me to enjoy the play on the stage, because of its humor and its circus quality, thanks to which the London production has been a general success with firstcomers. There are rumors that Mr. Beckett does not entirely approve of some of this horseplay at the bottom of his garden. If so, it confirms what I have already suggested about authors and the presentation of their own plays. Great thoughts alone do not catch the attention of the playgoing public, and when a dramatist breaks all the rules by having neither incident nor conflict in his first act, and then has the impertinence to give himself a full encore in his second, he need not be surprised if his play remains indefinitely with the Drama Leagues.

But this play, whether so intended or not, has a lot of the pantomime qualities of an Eggheads Harlequinade that makes it a delight from the start. It has Clown and Pantaloon, and Harlequin, and even the rich shopkeeper whose string of sausages is always disappearing. It does not come across as coterie stuff, unless deliberately played for pomposity or facetiousness. Its obscurities are largely superficial, and do not convey the impression that it is a Sphinx trying to conceal the fact that its creator has failed to provide it with any secret. We may not agree with its picture of life, but nobody can validly deny that there is a picture, and an arguable one.

Let us study for a moment the summing up of a day in the life of Vladimir, gray-matter-department of the double tramp that is presumably Beckett. Observe the timelessness of Time and how each day is the same as another—only different. Note how hard it sometimes is to be quite certain who one actually is, and whether one is asleep or awake. And finally, let us consider the strange and exciting similarity between Death and Birth that is so brilliantly underlined.

Was I sleeping while the others suffered? Am I sleeping now? Tomorrow, when I wake, or think I do, what shall I say of today? That with Estragon, my friend, at this place, until the fall of night, I waited for Godot? That Pozzo passed, with his carrier, and talked to us? Probably. But in all that what truth will there be? . . . [Estragon] will know nothing. He'll tell me about the blows he received and I'll give him a carrot. Astride of a grave and a difficult birth. Down in the hole, lingeringly, the grave-digger puts on the forceps. We have time to grow old. The air is full of our cries. But habit is a great deadener. At me too someone is looking, of me too someone is saying, He is sleeping, he knows nothing, let him sleep on. [p. 58a]

Maybe it is a lamentable fact that the Western world today does nothing but wait, enlivening the tedium, perhaps, with a little ambulance work. But lamentable or not, there is such a basis of truth in the picture that it seems reasonably certain that Waiting for Godot is destined to be the Play of the Fifties. In the Twenties and Thirties we were naive enough not to wait, but to search. And we know what we got. Hence a certain reluctance to investigate nowadays what may be just around the corner.

This is another reason for not examining this comb for any of Joyce's dandruff. Ulysses got around, and belongs to an earlier and (let us hope) a later generation. But Mr. Beckett is the suitor who has not only wooed, but successfully raped the patient Penelope—the patron saint of all waiters.

An Actor's Recollections

PETER BULL AS POZZO

PETER BULL

Rehearsals started soberly, and I took an instant liking to the young director Peter Hall, who made no bones about the play. "Haven't really the foggiest idea what some of it means," he announced cheerfully, "but if we stop and discuss every line we'll never open. I think it may be dramatically effective but there's no hope of finding out till the first night."

There was certainly no assistance coming from the author Mr. Samuel Beckett, and looking back on the production, I'm rather glad he didn't put in an appearance till quite late in the run. The rehearsals were the most gruelling that I've ever experienced in all my puff. The lines were baffling enough, but the props that I was required to carry about my person made life intolerable. Aspiring actors are hereby warned against parts that entail them being tied to another artiste, as they will find it restricts their movements. As well as this handicap I had to carry an overcoat, a giant watch, a pipe, lorgnettes, and heaven knows what else. The rope had to be adjusted continuously, so that I could pull it taut round my slave's neck, if possible not throttling Mr. Bateson (Lucky was the name of the character). Fortunately there were long duologues between the tramps, so while they rehearsed on the stage proper, Master Bateson and I could have a bash in the Oak Room of the Arts Club, until complaints came up, via the headwaiter from the restaurant below, about the noise and general banging about. It was wonderful weather (always is during rehearsals), and at lunch time I used to grab a sandwich or eight and dart off to the Oasis swimming pool. This brought back sanity with the chlorine and I was able to get through the afternoon. They were dreary days and evenings, as none of us, I think, dared to go out at night, owing to the necessity of getting the lines into our noodles. One of the main troubles was that an identical cue kept recurring every few pages of the script, so that it was remarkably easy to leave out whole chunks of the play. (We did, in fact, skip four pages on the actual first night at the Arts but, like fools, went back instead of pressing on.) In the second act I had to say "Help" about twenty times, a cue which didn't in fact help my fellow actors.

I found it frightfully difficult to get any sense out of my intended characterization, until the last weeks of rehearsals, when I suddenly decided to cheat and pretend Miss Margaret Rutherford was playing the role, which had the immediate and blessed effect of stopping embarrassing myself. It is a platitude to say that when an actor embarrasses himself, he is bound to embarrass the audience. I had noticed that my friends were clearly mortified at having to hear my lines, and Bob Morley had thrown the script from one end of his garden to the other, when I had unwisely asked him to take me through the part. The dress rehearsals were gloomy affairs and not relieved for yours truly by the physical discomforts of wearing a wig constructed of rubber, in the middle of a heat wave. Owing to the author's eccentricity it was necessary for Pozzo to take his bowler hat off at one stage of the piece and reveal a completely naked head. This was symbolic (the only explanation for the nightly torture given to me), and then he put his tifter on again. It was only for a second or two, but proved to be one of my major miseries. A firm of wig makers, Wig Creations Ltd., had constructed for me what amounted to a bathing cap, which had to be encased in rubber solution. This caused an impasse when dry, owing to lack of air in the hair, and by the end of any performance there were several pints of not madly attractive sweat accumulated in the rubber wig, which made one feel as if one's head had burst. Later in the run I contracted a series of skin diseases as a result and had to issue a *pronunciamento*. The consequence was that a new type of bathing cap was dished out, not so chic as it had a few wisps of hair at the back, which meant that I did not have to seal off my head completely. The whole thing was pretty preposterous because, as Mr. R. Morley kindly pointed out, the wig-join was clearly visible from Row K in the stalls. Make-up has never been my forte, and in this case the earlier I came in to do it, the more frightening seemed to be the result. I used to arrive some two hours before my first entrance in *Godot*, and by the time I reached the stage, the rubber had started to come unstuck, which resulted in ditto for my performance. If I ever got held up by necessity or accident and got into the theater late, I was always able to put on a superb make-up in ten minutes flat!

The first night was, I think, my most alarming experience on the stage (so far). I have a habit of comforting myself on first nights by trying to think of appalling experiences during the war, when terror struck from all sides, but the windiness felt on the Italian beachheads and elsewhere was nothing to compare with one's panic on that evening of August 3, 1955, and why the cast was not given medals of gallantry in the face of the enemy is inexplicable. Waves of hostility came whirling over the footlights, and the mass exodus, which was to form such a feature of the run of the piece, started quite soon after the curtain had risen. The audible groans were also fairly disconcerting. By the time I had to make my first entrance (twenty minutes after the rise of the curtain) I realized that I was in for a sticky evening and I'm not referring to my rubber wig. The laughs had been few and far between and there was a general air of restlessness and insecurity around. I lost my head quite early on by inserting the rope, by which Mr. Bateson was attached to me, *inside* my coat sleeve. Knowing what I do now and how the audience was never surprised by anything that happened during *Godot*, I should have just said, "Pig, put my coat on properly, pig," which was the endearing form of address that I habitually used to my slave.

As it was, I spent the next quarter of an hour in a semi-hysterical condition, knowing that if I hadn't actually strangled

Mr. Bateson by the time he got to make his big speech, it was highly probable that he would have to make it in pitch darkness owing to non-arrival at the position on which his spotlight was trained. As it was Mr. Bateson's big moment, I hazarded a guess that he might not be pleased. I gradually eased the rope up my sleeve in order to reduce the danger, but at the expense of my performance, which had by now been reduced to a question of survival without having heart failure. I was blowing the audience out of the auditorium with the volume of my shrill voice— (quote Kenneth Tynan) over-vocalization (unquote) which was the understatement of the year. But T. Bateson got his light, declaimed his gibberish and brought the house down with terrifying accuracy.

After this the audience were a little more attentive, and though an occasional groan or rudely upturned seat rang through the building, we got through without disaster. I pulled myself together in the second act and Messrs. Daneman and Woodthorpe were very moving indeed in the last scene of all. The curtain fell to mild applause, we took a scant three calls and a depression and sense of anticlimax descended on us all. Very few people came round, and most of those who did were in a high state of intoxication and made even less sense than the play. I slipped quietly away with the Scofields and Maurice Kaufmann, who had all promised to pick up the bits.

The notices next day were almost uniformly unfavorable, confused, and unprovocative. We played to poor houses, but on the Sunday following our opening the whole picture was to change. We quite suddenly became the rage of London, a phenomenon entirely due to the articles written by the Messrs. Tynan and Hobson in the *Observer* and *Sunday Times* respectively. One phrase quoted from each doyen of criticism was enough to send all London to the Arts and subsequently the Criterion theaters. Mr. Hobson said, "Something that will securely lodge in a corner of your mind as long as you live," and Mr. Tynan told his readers that "it will be a conversational necessity for many years to have seen *Waiting for Godot*."

With no mock humility I have to report that Mr. H. also said, "This Bull's bellow troubles the memory like the swan song of humanity," but I fancy Mr. Derek Granger in the *Financial Times* was nearer the mark when he said I looked like a "vast obscene baby."

The First Irish Director

PRODUCING *GODOT* IN DUBLIN

ALAN SIMPSON

When I first received the script from Sam Beckett, early in 1954, my immediate reaction was that the two tramps should be played as two Dublin characters. On reading a play the first time through, I always tend to hear it in my mind's ear as I hope it will be played and in the case of *Godot* I have never had any doubts as to the correctness for me at any rate, of this first impression.

The play as originally written in French contained a lot of subtleties which are inevitably lost in the English language even when translated by the author himself. One of the most important, for instance, is the very opening line, which is, *"Rien à faire."* Sam has translated this as, "Nothing to be done." Now this is obviously very important because, for the tramps, there *is* nothing to be done. But in French, this is a colloquialism, and can be thrown away with a sigh as just a little exclamation of tedium. In my original Dublin production I changed it to "It's no good," because I felt that it was more colloquial and less significant. However, I subsequently discussed it with Sam, and he was most emphatic that he wished it to be spoken as "Nothing to be done." I still think that this feeling should creep up on the audience unnoticeably, as it must do when spoken in French; but there seems to be no possible English equivalent.

45

When I reproduced the play recently at Theatre Workshop, some of the London critics attacked the concept of using a Dublin dialect for the tramps. Apart from my own personal feelings, there are other good reasons for doing this when playing the play in English. However, the personal feelings of the producer are very important, because if he has a particular conception of how the dialogue of any play should be spoken, obviously he will get the best results from following his own instincts. But there are more general reasons why I think a Dublin dialect is helpful to the fullest interpretation of the play.

When it was originally acted in French, the question of dialect didn't arise, because, by and large, there was no reason why the tramps should not speak perfect French. Accent in France is not a matter of class or education, except in the extremes of provincial patois or Parisian argot. In his English translation, Sam has used a number of long or erudite words, which would sound strange coming from the mouth of a Cockney, or even a Liverpudlian. If it is played with an Old Vic or Oxford accent, as Hugh Burden played it in the Criterion Theatre, London, one is immediately faced with the slight puzzlement of how someone so erudite could become such a scrofulous hobo. However, the Dubliner of humble circumstance, like his Negro or Indian counterpart, tends to use longer words and more elegant syntax than his educational level would seem to warrant by English standards. Thus for instance the line, "For the moment he's inert but he might run amuck any minute," sounds plausible in a Dublin voice, while the word "inert," coming from the mouth of an English tramp, would sound strange.

Dublin down-and-outs sometimes misuse long words, or use them in a slightly unusual way. So Vladimir's line, "But it's not for nothing I've lived through this long day and I can assure you it's very near the end of its repertory," although not in any way intrinsically Irish, flows very easily in the Dublin accent. There are, of course, throughout the play, a number of actual Dublinisms, such as Estragon's referring to Godot as "your man" and Vladimir's "I'd like well to hear him think," but this sort of thing is not of such great importance as the general tenor of Vladimir's phraseology. Estragon, being a simpler and less voluble character, can be quite convincing in any dialect, as was proved by the playing of the part by Peter Woodthorpe in broad Yorkshire, in the original Criterion production.

One English critic said of my recent production, "The language runs naturally into Irish cadences, but the trouble is that a good deal of it starts sounding like blarney." To me, at any rate, this is a good thing, if by "blarney" the critic means triviality. After all, Vladimir does remark in Act II: "This is becoming really insignificant." How many human beings go around discussing life in a significant way? Very few, I suspect, except perhaps in the more intense English plays, like those of John Whiting and Arnold Wesker.

"They give birth astride of a grave, the light gleams an instant, then it is night once more," is Samuel Beckett's view of a human life, as expressed through the mouth of Pozzo. When you consider the insignificance of the greatest or most famous human being as against the enormity of time and the universe, surely our most profound philosophies are as "blarney"?

My interpretation of the part of Pozzo is widely different from that of Roger Blin in France, and of any others I have heard about. The general reading of this character seems to be of an overbearing, bullying tycoon. Because of my own Irishness, however, I see him as an Anglo-Irish or English gentleman, whose excellent manners and superficially elaborate concern for others conceals an arrogant and selfish nature. The English upper classes are frequently horrified by the brutal treatment meted out by the other white races to their black or brown colonial possessions. But I believe that their own calm, almost unconscious assumption of superiority hurts and distresses these people even more than the downright bullying of others. . . .

The character of Lucky, on the other hand, I see in much the same terms as it was interpreted in France; a creature of ultimate degradation and suffering. The script is fairly specific about certain things. First of all Lucky must be in a state of physical debilitation so extreme that when Pozzo stops short on his first entrance, and tautens the rope, Lucky falls with all his baggage. Secondly, he must have long white hair.

The only aspect of Lucky not covered in the stage directions is his clothes. In this I followed Roger Blin's lead, by giving him a sort of old-fashioned footman's coat and knee breeches. There are in Ireland a number of Anglo-Irish aristocratic families, who live in grand, but excessively delapidated mansions, and it is not unusual for them to follow all the mores of their well-to-do English counterparts, without nearly enough money to do the thing properly. For this reason, I thought it would fit in with my conception of the Pozzo-Lucky relationship to have Lucky's elaborate livery moth-eaten and tattered. . . .

In attacking the long speech within the framework of Beckett's instructions, which are not particularly explicit at this point, I made the following suggestions. For the phrases with some sort of emotional connotation, I said that he should play them in a way that suggested the emotion implied in the words. For instance, "loves us dearly" was to be played sentimentally and softly; "plunged in torment, plunged in fire whose fire flames" in a manner suggesting extreme suffering; "heaven so blue still and calm so calm with a calm" drawn out, smoothly and gently; "the great cold the great dark" shiveringly, and so forth. In the linking passages, such as "which even though intermittent is better than nothing," he should speak quickly, in a dry manner suggestive of a caricatured university professor lecturing. I got him to vary the tempo in this way until the line "in the year of their Lord six hundred and something," after which he was to shout the lines as vigorously and rapidly as possible. The reactions of the tramps and Pozzo were to be as specifically outlined by Beckett, with the addition that the tramps should react shocked to "Fartov and Belcher," and "Feckham." I made the phrase, "the skull the skull the skull the skull" the signal for the all-out attack by the others in their efforts to stop the now frenzied spate of words. . . .

In Raymond Williams' review of this production in the *New Statesman*, he said:

Cut across by compulsion and fatigue as well as by the bab-
ble of scraps from the schoolmen and scientific scholarship,
this speech is still central. It is worth ignoring these scraps
and following the main line:

> Given the existence . . . of a personal God . . . who . . .
> loves us dearly with some exceptions for reasons unknown
> but time will tell and suffers . . . with those who . . . are
> plunged in torment . . . and considering . . . that . . . it
> is established beyond all doubt . . . that man . . . in spite
> of the strides . . . wastes and pines . . . and considering
> what is more much more grave . . . the great cold the great
> dark the air and the earth abode of stones in the great cold
> . . . alas alas on on . . . alas alas on on the skull the skull
> the skull . . .   [pp. 28a–29b]

This traditional vision of man's decline into death is confused and unfinished, on the edge of breakdown but not
broken down altogether, and the play was greatly strength-
ened by its clear speaking (the easy alternative is gabble
and horseplay).

I think the foregoing is quite a clever analysis of the speech,
but in this and in the rest of the play the actors and myself
never worried about the academic or philosophical implications
of the lines, but always followed our emotional instincts. Over
these, with both casts, we never seemed to have any doubts or
disagreements. The play has so many intellectual implications,
either intentional or accidental, that if actors and producers
were to try and approach their work on any sort of an academic
basis, it would lead to confusion and stilting of the easy flow of
the dialogue, which in my view is essential to any dramatic
performance. "Leave all that to the newspapermen," I used to
say, "they get paid for it, you get paid for acting."

The First American Director

WAITING FOR BECKETT:
A Personal Chronicle

ALAN SCHNEIDER

I take no sides. I am interested in the shape of ideas. There is a wonderful sentence in Augustine: "Do not despair; one of the thieves was saved. Do not presume; one of the thieves was damned." That sentence has a wonderful shape. It is the shape that matters.

—Samuel Beckett

In the three years that I have come to know him, the shape of Samuel Beckett as a human being has come to matter as much to me as do his plays. Perhaps even more. For Beckett is that most uncompromised of men, one who writes—and lives —as he must, and not as the world—and the world's critics— want him to. An artist, who works with no fears of "failure," which has fed him most of his writing life, or any expectation of "success," which has only lately greeted him. A friend, who has come unannounced to see me off at the Gare du Nord although I had not informed him which of the numerous trains to London I might be taking. The head of a physics or math professor set atop the torso and legs of a quarter-miler; a paradoxical combination of a Frenchman's fundamental "commitment" to life and an Irishman's basic good nature. Such is the shape of the man who has written some of the most terrifying and beautiful prose of the twentieth century.

From the *Chelsea Review*, No. 2, September, 1958, reprinted by permission of the author and *Chelsea Review*, where this material first appeared. This article has been abridged with the author's permission.

My first inkling of Beckett's existence came in Zurich, Switzerland, during the summer of 1954. A friend of mine at the Zurich *Schauspielhaus* urged me to look up a new play they had performed the previous season. It was called *Warten Auf Godot* and its French author had become the rage of intellectual Europe—though, of course, largely unrecognized in his Paris habitat, and unknown in English. When I arrived in Paris a few weeks later, I discovered, after much effort and many blank stares, that *En attendant Godot* was being presented at an off-beat Left Bank playhouse, the Théâtre de Babylone. Not quite sure what to expect, my wife and I went the following evening. The theater was tiny, the production extremely simple. There were nine people in the audience that first evening, a few more when we came again a night later. My French is just good enough to get me in and out of the American Express. Yet through the entire performance I sat alternately spellbound and mystified, knowing something terribly moving was taking place on that stage. When the highly stylized "moon" suddenly rose and night "fell" at the end of that first act, I didn't have to understand French in order to react. And when, at the beginning of the second act, the once-bare tree reappeared with little green ribbons for leaves, that simple representation of rebirth affected me beyond all reason. Without knowing exactly what, I knew that I had experienced something unique and significant in modern theater. *Godot* had me in the beginnings of a grip from which I have never escaped.

The next morning I tried to locate the author to see if the American rights were available. He had no phone, and no one would give me his home address. I left note after note, contacted everyone I could think of who might know—to no avail. Finally a friendly play agent informed me that the English-language rights had been acquired by a British director, Peter Glenville, who was planning to present the play in London with Alec Guinness as Vladimir and Ralph Richardson as Estragon. Besides, added the agent, the play was nothing an American audience would take—unless it could have a couple of top-flight comedians like Bob Hope and Jack Benny kidding it, preferably with Laurel and Hardy in the other two roles. An American production under those circumstances seemed hopeless, and Mr. Beckett as far removed as Mr. Godot himself. I came home to New York and went on to other matters.

The next spring (1955) I had occasion to remember once more. *Godot* received its English-language première in London, not with Guinness and Richardson at all but with a non-star cast at London's charming Arts Theatre Club. Damned without exception by the daily critics, it was hailed in superlatives by both Harold Hobson and Kenneth Tynan (the Atkinson and Kerr of London) in their Sunday pieces, and soon became the top conversation piece of the English season. At the same time, the English translation was published by Grove Press in New York, and began to sell an extraordinary number of copies not only in New York City but all over the United States. Everyone who could read was beginning to hear about this mysterious *Godot*.

I read and re-read the published version. Somehow, on its closely-spaced printed pages, it seemed cold and abstract, even harsh, after the remarkable ambience I had sensed at the Babylone. When a leading Broadway producer asked me what I thought of its chances, I responded only half-heartedly. Intrigued as I had been, I could not at the moment imagine a commercial production in Broadway terms.

One day in the fall of that same year, I was visiting my old alma mater, the University of Wisconsin, when to my utter amazement I received a long-distance phone call from producer Michael Myerberg asking me if I would be interested in directing *Waiting for Godot* in New York. He had Bert Lahr and Tom Ewell signed for the two main roles; and Thornton Wilder, whose *Skin of Our Teeth* I had directed for the Paris Festival that summer, had recommended me. It was like Fate knocking at the door. After a desperate search through practically every bookshop in Chicago, I finally located a copy, stayed up all night on the train studying it with new eyes, and arrived back in New York to breathe a fervent "yes" to Myerberg.

Followed a series of conferences with Lahr and Ewell, both of whom confessed their complete bewilderment with the play; and with Myerberg, who insisted that no one could possibly be bewildered, least of all himself. He did think it might be a good idea, however, for me to see the English production, perhaps stopping off on the way to have a talk with Beckett himself. To say that I was pleased and excited would be a pale reflection of the reality. And my elation was tempered only by the fear that Beckett would continue to remain aloof—he had merely reluctantly consented to a brief meeting with "the New York director."

At any rate, a week later I found myself aboard the U.S.S. Independence bound for Paris and London—and, by coincidence, the table companion and fellow conversationalist of Thornton Wilder, who was on his way to Rome and elsewhere. Crossing the Atlantic with Wilder was a stroke of good fortune and an experience I shall never forget. He greatly admired Beckett, considered *Godot* one of the two greatest modern plays (the other was, I believe, Cocteau's *Orpheus*), and openly contributed his ideas about an interpretation of the play, which he had seen produced in both French and German. In fact, so detailed and regular were our daily meetings that a rumor circulated that Wilder was rewriting the script, something which later amused both authors considerably. What was true was that I was led to become increasingly familiar with the script, both in French and in translation, and discovered what were the most important questions to ask Beckett in the limited time we were to have together. More specifically, I was now working in the frame of reference of an actual production situation—a three-week rehearsal period, a "tryout" in a new theater in Miami, and, of course, Bert and Tommy. It wasn't Bob Hope and Jack Benny, but that Parisian agent of two summers before had been correct so far. Was she also going to prove correct in terms of the audience response?

Beckett at that time had no phone—in fact, the only change I've noticed in him since his "success" is the acquisition of one—so I sent him a message by *pneumatique* from the very plush hotel near the Etoile where Myerberg had lodged me. Within an hour, he rang up saying he'd meet me in the lobby —at the same time reminding me that he had only half an hour or so to spare. Armed with a large bottle of Lacrima Christi, as a present from both Wilder and myself, I stationed myself in the rather overdone lobby and waited for the elusive Mr. Beckett to appear. Promptly and very business-like, he strode in, his tall athletic figure ensconced in a worn shortcoat; bespectacled in old-fashioned steel rims; his face as long and sensitive as a greyhound's. Greetings exchanged, the biggest question became where we might drink our Lacrima Christi; we decided to walk a bit and see if we could come up with a solution. Walk we did, as we have done so many times since, and talk as we walked—about a variety of matters including, occasionally, his play. Eventually, we took a taxi to his skylight apartment in the sixth *arrondissement* and wound up finishing most of the bottle. In between I plied him with all my studi-ously-arrived-at questions as well as all the ones that came to me at the moment; and he tried to answer as directly and as honestly as he could. The first one was "Who or what does Godot mean?" and the answer was immediately forthcoming: "If I knew, I would have said so in the play." Sam was perfectly willing to answer any questions of specific meaning or reference, but would not—as always—go into matters of larger or sym-bolic meanings, preferring his work to speak for itself and let-ting the supposed "meanings" fall where they may. . . .

Two days later, Sam came into London incognito, though some of the London newspapers, hearing rumors of his pres-ence, soon began searching for him. (To this day, he heartily dislikes interviews, cocktail parties, and all the other public concomitants of the literary life.) That night, and each night for the next five days, we went to see the production of *Godot*, which had been transferred by this time to the Criterion in Piccadilly Circus. The production was interesting, though scenically over-cluttered and missing many of the points which Sam had just cleared up for me. My fondest memories are of Sam's clutching my arm from time to time and in a clearly-heard stage whisper saying: "It's ahl wrahng! He's doing it ahl wrahng!" about a particular bit of stage business or the interpretation of a certain line. Every night after the performance, we would compare what we had seen to what he had intended, try to analyze why or how certain points were being lost, speak with the actors about their difficulties. Every night, also, we would carefully watch the audience, a portion of which always left during the show. I always felt that Sam would have been disappointed if at least a few hadn't.

Through all this, I discovered not only how clear and logical *Godot* was in its essences, but how human and how easy to know Sam was, how friendly beneath his basic shyness. I had met Sam, wanting primarily to latch on to anything which might help make *Godot* a success on Broadway. I left him, wanting nothing more than to please him. I came with respect; I left with a greater measure of devotion than I have ever felt for a writer whose work I was engaged in translating to the stage.

Though Sam felt he could not face the trials of the rehearsal and tryout periods, he promised to make his first trip to the United States once we had opened. As it turned out, he didn't —and we didn't. Of trials, however, there were plenty, somewhat above the usual quota. Doing *Godot* in Miami was, as Bert Lahr himself said, like doing *Giselle* in Roseland. Even though Bert and Tommy each contributed brilliantly comic and extremely touching performances, even though I felt more or less pleased with the production and felt that Sam would have been equally so, it was—in the words of the trade—a spectacular flop. The opening night audience in Miami, at best not too sophisticated or attuned to this type of material and at worst totally misled by advertising billing the play as "the laugh sensation of two continents," walked out in droves. And the so-called reviewers not only could not make heads or tails of the play but accused us of pulling some sort of a hoax on them. Although by the second week we were reaching—and holding— a small but devoted audience, the initial reception in Miami discouraged producer Myerberg, demoralized the cast, and led to the abandonment of the production. Later in the season, Myerberg changed his mind and brought *Godot* to Broadway, where it had a critical success; but the only member of the original company to go along was Bert Lahr, who gave substantially the same performance he had given in Miami (but this time without Tom Ewell to match him).

The failure in Miami depressed me more than any experience I had had in the theater, though I had from time to time anticipated its probability and done all in my power to avoid it. It is typical of Sam that his response to Miami was concerned only with my feelings of disappointment, and never stressed or even mentioned his own.

THE TALENT OF SAMUEL BECKETT

ERIC BENTLEY

The minute a statement was released to the press that Beckett's *Waiting for Godot* was not for casual theatergoers but for intellectuals, I could have written Walter Kerr's review for him. And I felt myself being jockeyed into writing a defense of the play as if by its success or failure civilization would stand or fall. Such is criticism.

Or is it? Besides the intellectual anti-intellectualism of a Walter Kerr, two other attitudes, both of them less objectionable, have defined themselves in modern America: one is non-intellectual pro-intellectualism and the other is non-intellectual anti-intellectualism. Both these attitudes were represented in the newspaper reviews of *Waiting for Godot,* and obviously the production benefited as much from the first as it suffered from the second. Both groups of critics found the writing beyond them. The first was prepared to be respectful toward what was not fully understood. The second joined Mr. Kerr in finding something of a scandal in the very existence of difficulty. And there emerged, in his review and theirs, one of the big ideas of the century:

Thinking is a simple, elementary process. Godot is merely a stunt . . .

—John Chapman, The Daily News

The author was once secretary to that master of obfuscation, James Joyce. Beckett appears to have absorbed some of his employer's ability to make the simple complex . . .

—Robert Coleman, The Daily Mirror

From the *New Republic*, May 14, 1956, reprinted by permission of the author.

... the rhythms of an artist [Bert Lahr] with an eye to God's own truth. All of them, I think, are the rhythms of musical comedy, or revue, of tanbark entertainment—and they suggest that Mr. Lahr has, all along in his own lowbrow career, been in touch with what goes on in the minds and hearts of the folk out front. I wish that Mr. Beckett were as intimately in touch with the texture of things.

—Walter Kerr, New York Herald Tribune

The superior insight of genius is unnecessary. All we need, to take upon us the non-mystery of things, is constant communion with the man of non-distinction.

Speaking of obfuscation, what could obfuscate our experience of Beckett's play more than the cloud of conflict between highbrow and lowbrow, highbrow and highbrow, lowbrow and lowbrow? This conflict is, of course, anterior to the play. The play itself presents a problem for our audiences too, and that is the problem of nausea as a playwright's conscious attitude to life.

Though it is permissible to be nauseated by existence, and even to say so, it seems doubtful whether one should expect to be paid for saying so, at any rate by a crowd of people in search of an amusing evening. Yet, since the humor which provides amusement is precisely, as Nietszche observed, a victory over nausea, it would be hard to stage the victory without at least suggesting the identity and character of the foe. It has taken Krafft-Ebbing and Freud to force a general admission of the importance of nausea even, say, in the work of Swift, where it is most prominent.

American optimism drives American nausea a little more deeply underground: that is the difference between America and Europe. For, if the conscious "thought" of "serious" literature and drama becomes more insistently "positive," a nation's humor, arising from the depths of discomfort, repression, and guilt, will become more and more destructive. Even now, if there is nothing quite so happy-drunk as American confidence, there is also nothing quite so blackly despondent as American

cynicism, the "hardboiledness" of the "tough guy." But the
ranks of the community close in order to hide the fact. Hence
the great loathing and fear of any more conscious type of
pessimism, such as that which flows in a steady stream from
France. For Broadway use, the professional pessimism of
Anouilh is made over into professional idealism.

Samuel Beckett's point of view seems pretty close to that of
Anouilh or Sartre. *Waiting for Godot* is, so to speak, a play
that one of them ought to have written. It is the quintessence
of "existentialism" in the popular, and most relevant, sense of
the term—a philosophy which underscores the incomprehensi-
bility, and therefore the meaninglessness, of the universe, the
nausea which man feels upon being confronted with the fact
of existence, the praiseworthiness of the acts of defiance man
may perform—acts which are taken, on faith, as self-justifying,
while, rationally speaking, they have no justification because
they have no possibility of success.

Like many modern plays, *Waiting for Godot* is undramatic
but highly theatrical. Essential to drama, surely, is not merely
situation but situation in movement, even in beautifully shaped
movement. A *curve* is the most natural symbol for a dramatic
action, while, as Aristotle said, beginning, middle, and end are
three of its necessary features. Deliberately anti-dramatic,
Beckett's play has a shape of a non-dramatic sort; two strips of
action are laid side by side like railway tracks. These strips are
One Day and the Following Day in the lives of a couple of
bums. There *cannot* be any drama because the author's conclusion is that the two days are the same. That there are also things
that change is indicated by a play-within-this-play which also
has two parts. The first time that the characters of the inner
play come on they are a brutal Master and his pitiful Man; the
second time they are both equally pitiful because the Master
has gone blind.

What has brought the play before audiences in so many
countries—aside from snobberies and phony publicity—is its
theatricality. Highbrow writers have been enthusiastic about
clowns and vaudeville for decades, but this impresses me as the

first time that anything has successfully been done about the matter. Mr. Kerr gave Bert Lahr all the credit for a traditional yet rich characterization, which, however, had been skillfully put together by Mr. Beckett. The author, to recapitulate, has not only been able to define the "existentialist" point of view more sharply than those who are more famously associated with it, he has also found for its expression a vehicle of a sort that people have been recommending without following their own recommendation.

It is, therefore, an important play. Whether it is more important than these two achievements suggest is the question. To me, the play did not come over with the force of revelation, nor with that of sheer greatness. Mr. Beckett's voice is interesting, but one does not quite find it individual, because it does not quite seem new. One is surely not exploiting an external fact unfairly in saying that Mr. Beckett is excessively—if quite inevitably—over-influenced by Joyce. If Russian literature is cut from Gogol's *Overcoat*, Irish literature is cut from those coats of many colors, *Ulysses* and *Finnegans Wake*.

I do not think the play is obscure except as any rich piece of writing is obscure. No doubt there are meanings that will disengage themselves in time as one lives with such a work, yet enough is clear from the first not only to arouse interest but to communicate a sense of a unified and intelligible image of life. I take it that Beckett belongs to that extensive group of modern writers who have had a religious upbringing, retain religious impulses and longings, but have lost all religious belief. I should differentiate him from, say, Sartre, in that he does not write from the standpoint of atheism but, theologically speaking, from that of skepticism. People who have seen *Godot* are able to suggest this or that solution—Christian, anti-Christian, etc.— precisely because Beckett has left the door open for them to do so. They are wrong only if they intimate that the author himself passed through the door and closed it behind him. Rough words have been spoken about the allegedly excessive symbolism of the play. This is unjust. Beckett's finest achievement is to have made the chief relationships, which are many, so concrete that abstract interpretations are wholly relegated to the theater lobby. He gives us, not tenets, but alternatives seen as human relationships (between bum and bum, master and man); also as ordinary human attitudes to God, Nature, and Death on the one hand, and, on the other, to the "trivialties," such as clothes, defecation, smells . . .

The New York production is so good that I can dispose of the only serious shortcomings in a few lines. The lighting is of that "modern" sort which is now old-fashioned and was always awful: you don't see the actors' faces properly, and every time an actor moves he is either moving into much less light or much more. One of the actors seems miscast. This is Kurt Kasznar as Pozzo, the Master, who gave us a playful stage villain instead of a stomach-turning real one; Mr. Kasznar was so brilliant as the Director in *Six Characters* that he has been lured into repeating part of the characterization in a very different role.

On the first night, Alvin Epstein as Lucky, the Man, threw away the content of the most effective speech in the play, into which Beckett seems to have poured all his training in Catholic philosophy. At the second performance, which I also attended, the fault had largely been corrected, without detriment to the pantomime, which is Mr. Epstein's specialty. E. G. Marshall, as one of the bums, was overshadowed by his partner. His acting seemed to me defensive—and therefore, as things work out on the stage, a little self-destructive. The part was under-acted—sometimes almost to the point of inaudibility. Long speeches were attacked diffidently with the usual result: that they constantly seemed to be over before they were, and one thought: Heavens, is he starting up again? Yet all this is by no means as disastrous as spelling it out makes it sound. In any part, Mr. Marshall is interesting.

Estragon, the less philosophical bum, the *dummer August* of this particular circus, is played by Bert Lahr. If to Mr. Kerr this fact just means the saving of a highbrow play by a lowbrow actor, it is just as fair to look upon it as the perfect execution by a lowbrow actor of a highbrow writer's intentions. If the perfection of it is bound to hurt the less perfect impersonations by contrast, it has the merit of enabling us to visualize a perfect production of the play as a whole and even, by extension, a perfect play of this type perfectly produced.

We sentimentalize vaudeville now, and overrate it; go back to the reports of William Archer and Bernard Shaw, and you'll find it was usually atrocious. I shall not insult Mr. Lahr by giving the credit for his work to an institution that did not in fact have very high standards. That he acquired certain habits is all to the good though there are plenty of actors with those habits who would have failed in *Godot*. The triumph here is partly due to his bringing to the script a respect which has not been shared by all the commentators on it. One does see the advantage of his training, for, while Mr. Marshall has to create a clown and constantly work at it, Mr. Lahr did his creating in that line so long ago that he settles and relaxes into a clown personality as others do into a smoking jacket and carpet slippers. He reminds me strongly of Menasha Skulnik in *The Flowering Peach*. On both occasions, literature and popular comedianship met. But it was a matter of marriage, not lifesaving. Both actors showed respect for the words they spoke, while the words, gratefully, but with a proper pride, gave something to the actor that made him larger and richer than he had been, perhaps ever, before.

Herbert Berghof directed. I have less reverence for this play than he, and would have lopped off the last bit of the first act. I would also have been tempted to make cuts at several points where the dialogue stumbles. (The rhythm is very firm for longish stretches but will from time to time just go to pieces.) But reverence toward a script is a good fault, and, on Broadway, an unusual, almost exemplary, one.

Though many directors have their characteristic tricks, or their famous and much-publicized manner, very few give to their shows the imprint of an individual human being. This imprint Mr. Berghof—in the quietest way in the world—imparts. In a brief commentary, one has to point to particular touches—such as the delicate way one bum takes the other's thumb out of his mouth while he sleeps, or the soft and stealthy way in which Mr. Lahr would curl up and go to sleep, or the confident way in which one actor or the other would undertake moves which the realistic directors don't use (such as walking in a circle). But Mr. Berghof's personality—gentle, sensitive, youthful, fanciful—is not found only in the "blocking" and stage business; it is far more subtly interfused and, with the co-operation of the actors, gives the evening its special aroma and dignity.

A remark—perhaps irrelevant—about the title. "Godot" is the person you are waiting for who, presumably, will set things to rights when he arrives. I assume that Mr. Beckett made up the French word from the English one, God. But, as someone will no doubt inform *The Times Literary Supplement*, there is a once well-known play of Balzac's in which we spend the whole evening waiting for a character called Godeau, who has still not come on stage when his arrival is announced just before the final curtain falls.

Postscript 1967

My *New Republic* review of eleven years ago records my first impressions of *Godot*. "No doubt," I wrote, "there are meanings that will disengage themselves in time, as one lives with such a work." And, in fact, with time I ceased to believe that the play was "undramatic" and only "theatrical," and I set down my later belief—that *Godot* is truly dramatic—in my book *The Life of the Drama* (New York: Atheneum, 1964, pp. 99–101 and 348–351). My early reading of Beckett missed out an essential element both dramatic and ... I might even blame the error, in part, on Beckett himself, in that his English title does not translate the much more apt French one: *En attendant Godot*, which means "*while* waiting for Godot." The subject is not that of pure waiting. It is: what happens in certain human beings *while* waiting. Estragon and Vladimir do not only wait. *In* waiting they show, ultimately, human dignity: *they* have kept their appointment, even if Godot has not. A lot of comment on Beckett goes wrong in taking for granted a pessimism more absolute than *Godot* embodies, in other words in taking for granted that Godot will not come. This philosophical mistake produces a mistake in dramatic criticism, for to remove the element of uncertainty and suspense is to remove an essential tension—in fact the essential drama.

So much for the insufficiency of my earlier comments on the play. As for its historic destiny, it is summed up in Polish critic Jan Kott's answer to a questioner who asked: "What is the place of Bertolt Brecht in your [i.e., the Polish] theater?" He said: "We do him when we want Fantasy. When we want Realism, we do *Waiting for Godot*." This remark might also bring to mind the comment of the English poet and critic, Al Alvarez: "The real destructive nihilism acted out in the [extermination] camps was expressed artistically only in works like Beckett's *Endgame* or *Waiting for Godot*, in which the naked unaccommodated man is reduced to the role of helpless, hopeless, impotent comic, who talks and talks and talks in order to postpone for a while the silence of his own desolation." It is the historic destiny of *Waiting for Godot* to represent the "waiting" of the prisoners of Auschwitz and Buchenwald, as also the prisoners behind the walls and barbed wire of Walter Ulbricht, as also the prisoners behind the spiritual walls and barbed wire of totalitarian society generally, as also the prisoners behind the spiritual walls and barbed wire of societies nearer home. I would add to Alvarez's observation that, in this waiting, there is not only an adjustment to desolation, there is a rebuff to desolation. Even the Auschwitz prisoners hoped, however improbably, to get out: it is not certain that Godot *won't* come. And what Beckett's work ultimately embodies is this hope. Which again might be contained within the definition of what Kott playfully calls Realism. For, whether they should or not, people do continue to hope for Godot's arrival.

MANKIND IN THE MERDECLUSE

HENRY HEWES

The American theatergoer is apt to find *Waiting for Godot* an exasperating play whose allegories fascinate but never quite decipher. He may also find its lack of plot and its long patches of seemingly unremarkable dialogue a pale compensation for sitting two hours in the theater.

But for *Godot* supporters these very deficiencies seem its greatest virtues. Irish expatriate Samuel Beckett sets his play in the Vaucluse section of the unoccupied zone of France during World War II. In the middle of this bleak limbo sit two tramps, Vladimir and Estragon. They are waiting for a mysterious Mr. Godot (God) who has promised to meet them there. Along comes a well-dressed European landowner named Pozzo (Capitalist-Aristocrat) followed by a wretched, exhausted slave named Lucky (Labor-Proletariat) whom he leads by means of a long towrope tied around the neck. Then comes an entertainment in which Lucky is forced to perform an agonized, convulsive dance, and to give a demonstration of "thinking," in which he runs together a series of phrases expressing man's confusion as a result of having accepted "a personal god with a white beard outside time without extension." After this pair depart, one of Godot's two sons shows up to inform Vladimir, whom he calls Mr. Albert—(Schweitzer?), that Mr. Godot won't come this evening but will surely come tomorrow.

The next day (we assume World War II has passed during the night because the dead tree has sprouted a few leaves) Estragon returns to Vladimir to report he has been beaten by ten assailants. After more conversation Pozzo (now blind) stumbles in still leading Lucky (now dumb, "he can't even groan"). Pozzo asks them to help him up again. And the two tramps decide this is a more prudent course of action than

From the *Saturday Review*, May 5, 1956, reprinted by permission.

helping Lucky, because Pozzo is the only one who can keep Lucky from running amuck. Pozzo and Lucky leave again and the same boy (who we assume is Mr. Godot's other son) shows up with the same message as before. He also informs Vladimir that Godot has a white beard. Vladimir falls to his knees crying, "Christ have mercy upon us." Estragon suggests dropping Godot, but Vladimir refuses because "He'd punish us." So they decide to hang themselves *unless* Godot comes tomorrow, in which case Vladimir stoutly maintains they would be saved.

Mr. Beckett has sprinkled his tea with mysterious allusions. His Vladimir likes the New Testament Gospels and is loaded with anxiety about the fact that only one apostle mentioned that one of the two thieves crucified with Jesus was saved. The less inquisitive Estragon likes the Old Testament with its map of the Holy Land where he had once planned to go on his honeymoon. Vladimir is constantly saving Estragon from suicide attempts and persecution. But Vladimir refuses to listen to Estragon's nightmares, and upbraids him for not being ashamed to ask money for services rendered and for whiningly blaming the world for his own misery. Vladimir points out to Estragon that he is beaten not for what he does but for the way he does it. Despite the knowledge that each functions better separately they find themselves bound together. The same unhappy marriage exists with Pozzo and Lucky. And this suggests that *Waiting for Godot* is primarily concerned with the basic human problem of dualism, whether it be psychic, religious, social, or economic. The last fifty years' widespread acceptance of the ideas of Freud and Marx has decreased man's individuality and dignity and tended to make him the pawn of paired opposing opposite forces without and within.

Though these interesting ideas and many more emerge from the American production of *Waiting for Godot*, the actors seem to accept the play more as fancy than as fact. While Bert Lahr brings both pathos and his own brand of pretension-puncturing humor to Estragon, he too often punctures the pretensions of the play itself. E. G. Marshall plays Vladimir in a consciously intellectual manner, and his embrace of Estragon becomes merely symbolic. Kurt Kasznar's Pozzo emerges rather more of a villain than even a capitalist need be. Alvin Epstein's Lucky is a compelling and expert performance and seems closest of all to the spirit of the play.

Herbert Berghof's direction uses some expressionistic techniques and keeps the vitality-level high on-stage. Keeping it high in the audience is another matter. There Mr. Beckett's skeletal synthesis of postwar European despair engenders less dramatic excitement than it provokes post-theater discussion.

A PUBLIC NOTICE ON *WAITING FOR GODOT*

NORMAN MAILER

It is never particularly pleasant for me to apologize, and in the present circumstances I loathe doing so. To announce a farewell appearance and then be on the scene again the following week is to ooze all the ebbing charm and reeking sweat of the desperate old actor or the failing middle-aged bullfighter who simply cannot let go, cannot disappear, even if it is for no more than to hear some new catcalls, and conceivably get gored.

Since I have my pride, I would have preferred to keep my word and not appear again in this newspaper unless and until its general policy would change. But I have a duty to my honesty as well, and I did something of which I am ashamed, and so must apologize in the hardest but most meaningful way:— by public advertisement.

I am referring of course to what I wrote about *Waiting for Godot* in my last column. Some of you may remember that I

From *Advertisements for Myself* (New York: G. P. Putnam's Sons, 1959), copyright © 1959 by Norman Mailer. Reprinted by permission. The article originally appeared in *The Village Voice*, May 7, 1966.

said Beckett's play was a poem to impotence and appealed
precisely to those who were most impotent. Since then I have
read the play, seen the present Broadway production, read the
play again, have thought about it, wrestled with its obscurities
(and my conscience), and have had to come up reluctantly
with the conviction that I was most unfair to Beckett. Because
Waiting for Godot is a play about impotence rather than an
ode to it, and while its view of life is indeed hopeless, it is an
art work, and therefore, I believe, a good. While I think it is
essentially a work of a minor artist because its range of life-
experience is narrow if deep, it is all the same, whether major or
minor, the work of a man who has conscientiously and with
great purity made the uncompromising effort to abstract his
view of life into an art work, no matter how unbearable that
view of life may be. It is bad enough and sad enough when the
critics of any given time attack an artist and fail to understand
him, but then this is virtually to be taken for granted. For an
artist to attack another, however, and to do it on impulse, is a
crime, and for the first time in months I have been walking
around with a very clear sense of guilt.

Oddly enough, in superficial ways, and without reading
Godot, I was on the target in what I wrote last week. As I type
this now—it is Sunday—there is an interview with Samuel
Beckett in the *Times* drama section written by Israel Shenker,
and I wish to quote from it. Beckett says at one point:

> The kind of work I do is one in which I'm not master of
> my material. The more Joyce knew the more he could. He's
> tending toward omniscience and omnipotence as an artist.
> I'm working with impotence, ignorance. I don't think im-
> potence has been exploited in the past. There seems to be a
> kind of aesthetic axiom that expression is an achievement—
> must be an achievement. My little exploration is that whole
> zone of being that has always been set aside by artists as
> something unuseable—as something by definition incom-
> patible with art.
>
> I think anyone nowadays who pays the slightest attention

to his own experience finds it the experience of a non-knower, a non-can-er (somebody who cannot). The other type of artist—the Apollonian—is absolutely foreign to me.

Fair enough and honest enough—it elicits one's respect. What still distresses me and distresses Beckett as well, I would guess, is that *Godot* has become the latest touchstone in social chi-chi, and people who don't have the faintest idea of what he is talking about, and who as they watch the play, scream and gurgle and expire with a kind of militant exacerbated snobbery, are exactly the majority of people who have promoted *Godot* here. Because not to like *Waiting for Godot* is to suffer damnation—one is no longer chic.

(As a long parenthesis, I must add that it is impossible to understand the play without reading it, because the present production is in my opinion abominable: insensitive, hammy, sentimental, and pretentious in every wrong way—the acting is equally misleading. Only Alvin Epstein who plays Lucky gives an exciting and illuminating performance—the other actors merely flatten characterization into caricature.)

Most of the present admirers of *Godot* are, I believe, snobs, intellectual snobs of undue ambition and impotent imagination, the worst sort of literary type, invariably more interested in being part of some intellectual elite than in the creative act itself. This combination almost always coincides with a sex-hater, for if one is ashamed of sex or is unhappy with sex, then the next best thing is to rise in the social world. But since people with poor sexual range seldom have the energy and the courage to rise imaginatively or defiantly, they obligatorily give themselves to the escalator of the snob which is slow but ultimately sure of some limited social ascension.

And for these reasons I assumed in advance that *Godot* was essentially and deeply anti-sexual, and I was wrong. It has almost no sexual hope within it, but that is its lament, that is Beckett's grief, and the comic tenderness of the story comes from the resignation of that grief. So far as it is a story, it is a sad little story, but told purely.

Two men, two vagabonds, named Vladimir and Estragon (Didi and Gogo), a male and female homosexual, old and exhausted, have come to rest temporarily on a timeless plain, presided over by a withered cross-like tree, marooned in the purgatory of their failing powers. Their memories have become uncertain as vapors, their spirits are broken, they cannot even make love to each other any longer, they can only bicker and weep and nag and sulk and sleep, they are beyond sex, really neither old men nor old women but debilitated children looking for God, looking for the Life-Giver. They are so desperate they even speak wanly of hanging themselves, because this at least will give them one last erection. But they have not the power to commit suicide, they are exhausted and addled by the frustration of their failures to the point where they cannot even commit a despairing action. They can only wait for Godot, and they speculate feebly about his nature, for Godot is a mystery to them, and after all they desire not only sex and rebirth into life, but worldly power as well. They are looking for the potency of the phallus and the testes. Vladimir speaks of the Savior and the Two Thieves, and how one of the thieves was saved. The implication is that he and Gogo are withered puffballs, balls blown passively through life, opportunistic and aimless as small thieves, perhaps one of them and only one may be saved, and he is tempted: perhaps he is the one. Which would be of course at the expense of his life-mate Gogo. So in the religious sense he is not even pure in despair, but is already tempted into Sin.

Enter Pozzo and Lucky: Pozzo the fat gentleman with the whip and the rope around the neck of Lucky his slave, his wretch, the being at the mercy of his will. Pozzo dominates Lucky, abuses him, commands him about like a cruel brain abusing its own body.

And Vladimir has his opportunity for action, he can rescue Lucky, indeed he protests at the treatment of Lucky. But Vladimir, like Gogo, is seduced by the worldly power of Pozzo,

or at the very least in aiding Pozzo to beat Lucky into unconsciousness at the end of his single, impassioned speech.

Thereafter, the action (what there is of it) descends, and
when Pozzo and Lucky reappear, Pozzo is blind and Lucky is
dumb—we will hear his wisdom no longer. Their condition is
even more debased than Gogo's and Didi's. But for some will
remain the echo of Lucky's speech.

It is the one strangled cry of active meaning in the whole
play, a desperate retching pell-mell of broken thoughts and in-
tuitive lunges into the nature of man, sex, God, and time, it
comes from a slave, a wretch, who is closer to the divine than
any of the other characters, it is a cry across the abyss from
impotence to Apollo (Dionysius is indeed quite beyond the
horizon) and Pozzo, Gogo, and Didi answer the cry by beating
Lucky into unconsciousness. Thereafter, Lucky—the voice, the
midwife to the rebirth of the others—is stricken dumb, for he
too suffers from failing powers, he too is overcome by the succession of his defeats and so brought closer to death. Later,
much later, at the end of the play, Vladimir talks to the boy
who brings the message that Godot will not come that day, and
as Vladimir questions him about Godot, the boy says that
Godot has a white beard. But Lucky, who has a head of white
hair, had begun his speech (which again is the intellectual lock
and key of the play) by talking of "a personal God quaquaquaqua with white beard . . ." exactly the speech which the others
had destroyed. So Vladimir has a moment of agony: "Christ
have mercy on us!" he says to the boy. Through vanity, through
cupidity, through indifference, through snobbery itself, Vladimir
and Gogo have lost the opportunity to find Godot—they have
abused the link which is Lucky. (I must say that I am not
altogether unconvinced that Lucky himself may be Godot—it
is, at the least, a possibility.) At any rate, Vladimir and Gogo
have failed still again, their condition is even more desperate,
and so the play ends. "Yes, let's go," says Gogo in the final line,
but Beckett follows with the stage direction: *They do not
move. Curtain.*

It is possible that consciously or unconsciously Beckett is restating the moral and sexual basis of Christianity which was lost with Christ—that one finds life by kissing the feet of the poor, by giving of oneself to the most debased corners of the most degraded, that as the human condition in the world is to strive, no matter how cruelly, to rise to the top, so life and strength come from adoring the bottom for that is where God conceals himself.

Yet, there is another and richer possibility. For I believe Beckett is also saying, again consciously or unconsciously, that God's destiny is flesh and blood with ours, and so, far from conceiving of a God who sits in judgment and allows souls, lost souls, to leave purgatory and be born again, there is the greater agony of God at the mercy of man's fate, God determined by man's efforts, man who has free will and can no longer exercise it and God therefore in bondage to the result of man's efforts. At the end, Vladimir and Gogo have failed again, there is the hint, the murmur, that God's condition is also worse, and he too has come closer to failure—when Vladimir asks the boy in the closing minutes of the play what Godot does, the boy answers: "He does nothing, Sir." Godot, by implication, lives in the same condition, the same spiritual insomnia, agony, limbo, the same despair of one's fading powers which has hung over the play.

THE LONG WAIT FOR GODOT

ALAN LEVY

Who or what is the unseen Godot? To some he is death; to others, life; to a few, nothing. To one British critic, Kenneth

From *Theatre Arts*, August, 1956, copyright © 1956 by National Theatre Arts Council. Reprinted by permission of the author and his agent, Theron Raines.

Tynan, he is a "spiritual signpost." To the director of the Miami production, Godot is the meaning of life. To the man sitting next to me in London, he was beauty. Harvey Breit of *The New York Times Book Review* said: "This is Hell, upper case—and lower case, too." Then he added: "This is life." In the same newspaper, drama critic Brooks Atkinson said: "It seems fairly certain that Godot stands for God." *Time's* reviewer wasn't sure if Godot stands for God or man's unconquerable hope. He wasn't even sure if the play is "a philosophic depth bomb or a theatrical dud." When the director of the first American production asked Beckett what the mysterious Godot symbolized, the playwright replied: "If I knew what Godot was, I would have said so." . . .

Both the Paris and London productions of *Waiting for Godot* were flukes, according to Alan Schneider, director of the ill-fated Miami production. Schneider inspected the Paris and London versions and later met Beckett in Paris. "The Paris production," he reported, "was done in a very small theater and, while it was popular, it didn't set Paris on fire or anything. Why, only last year, I mentioned it to a French producer who's the Paris equivalent of—say—Gilbert Miller, and she'd never heard of *Waiting for Godot*. It always required a very special audience and it always had a very special audience in Europe. It was a more sophisticated, more philosophical crowd than what you'd get in Miami or on Broadway." . . .

In Miami, however, critic Jack Anderson of the *Herald* found Godot neither funny nor successful. He said he "almost felt sorry for the first-night audience," which was "sandbagged by an allegory." And the correspondent from *Variety* definitely proved no *godotista*. "The import from London," he reported, "is a wearisome two-acter, aimless in plotting, devoid of excitement, an impossible guessing game containing little to keep a theatergoer interested." He found the casting "a deplorable waste of talent" and the script full of "double-talk inanities." On opening night, fully 40 per cent of the audience concurred and walked out on the play. For two weeks Miami cabbies referred to the Coconut Grove Playhouse as the place where they picked up their fares after the first act.

I felt like an undertaker when I launched my investigation of the apparent American demise of *Godot* in Miami. Three days after the first production folded, I telephoned Tom Ewell in Greenwich, Connecticut. Ewell, who previously had been identified with *The Seven Year Itch* on stage and screen, was Vladimir during the two weeks in Miami. He and Bert Lahr, who played Estragon, were starred. Lahr was the only member of the cast retained for the Broadway resuscitation of *Godot*. Ewell was replaced by E. G. Marshall. "I'd rather not talk about it," Ewell said. "I'm terribly upset." He sounded terribly upset. He added: "*Godot* is one of the great plays of our time; it still is. I think it's the most universal play of the last twenty years." Then what went wrong? Ewell wasn't sure. He thought it might have been the choice of Miami as the break-in point. He said he conceived of *Godot*'s setting as "the limbo between life and death." Fashionable Miami, during the winter vacation season, is the last place to depict such an existence, Ewell suggested. . . .

In early April, an advertisement appeared in the drama sections of the New York newspapers. It announced that *Godot* was coming to Broadway for a limited engagement. And a signed postscript by Meyerberg warned: "I respectfully suggest that those who come to the theater for casual entertainment do not buy a ticket to this attraction." Bert Lahr had turned down several offers in order to remain available for another chance at Estragon, his first strictly dramatic role. A baffled interviewer asked the veteran comedian what the play is about. "Damned if I know," Lahr confessed.

After months of waiting the New York critics were ready for *Godot*. Some of them liked the play, and most of those who didn't acted hospitable. They left it to the individual reader to decide if *Godot* was his meat or poison. John Chapman of the *Daily News* called it "the most novel theatrical novelty since *The Skin of Our Teeth*." And John McClain conceded in the *Journal-American* that *Godot* is "a fantastically nonconformist evening in the theater" with "a madness that will make it conversation fodder." But there was also positive thinking about *Godot*. Richard Watts, Jr. of the *Post* used such phrases as "continuously fascinating," "moving," "grotesquely beautiful," and "utterly absorbing." Brooks Atkinson of the *Times* found in Beckett a "strange power . . . to convey the impression of some melancholy truths about the hopeless destiny of the human race." Atkinson concluded: "Although *Waiting for Godot* is a 'puzzlement,' as the King of Siam would express it, Mr. Beckett is no charlatan. He has strong feelings about the degradation of mankind, and he has given vent to them occasionally. *Waiting for Godot* is all feeling. Perhaps that is why it is puzzling and convincing at the same time. Theatergoers can rail at it, but they cannot ignore it. For Mr. Beckett is a valid writer."

Perhaps the most savage railing came from Mark Barron of the Associated Press, who sent this report on *Waiting for Godot* to hundreds of newspapers: "Probably the craziest play in years. . . . It is in that confused school of playwriting introduced by James Joyce and Gertrude Stein . . . *Waiting for Godot* is difficult to understand because the dialogue is confusing, the performers are obviously doing double talk to cover their own conversational meandering, and there is no sense at all to the whole production." Barron thought the plot was "about a group of people waiting for Godot, apparently a secret agent, to come and free them to cross a forbidden border. But Godot, their one chance of escape, never arrives." He concluded that "Bert Lahr should return to musical comedies and *Waiting for Godot* should take a quiet sleep." But most of the critics behaved like the first-nighter who said: "I'm not sure I understand it, but I'm trying hard. Really I am."

Waiting for Godot has been "adopted" by three Pulitzer Prize playwrights—Tennessee Williams, Thornton Wilder, and William Saroyan. Williams regards *Godot* as one of the greatest plays of modern times and invested in Meyerberg's productions. Wilder saw the play five times in Europe. Saroyan, according to the *New York Times*, all but weeps with emotion when he speaks of *Godot*. "It will make it easier for me and everyone else to write freely in the theater."

Beckett never expected his play to go as far as it has. His attitude is as cryptic as his play. When director Schneider warned him that the public might not comprehend the play's ideas, he replied: "If they don't understand it, the hell with them."

DIALOGUE: THE FREE SOUTHERN THEATRE

SCHECHNER: What about *Godot*?

MOSES: What about *Godot*?

SCHECHNER: I remember our discussions last Fall. We decided to do *Purlie*—which I now think was a mistake—and we tried to find the other play: *Blues for Mister Charlie, Godot, Antigone, The Mother.* And we picked *Godot* . . .

MOSES: We wanted to see what would happen. We chose it because it's a great play, and we thought *Godot* would act as a barometer of the limits, the ceiling of this audience. It didn't operate that way. All we learned was that our audience can take *Godot*.

SCHECHNER: How did people react?

MOSES: Let's talk about the kids. They were fascinated. In Ruleville, the morning before *Godot*, we held a drama workshop and did improvisations with about thirty kids. They enjoyed it tremendously. In this group was a kid named Jerry Johnson who has remarkable sensitivity. After the play that night he and a friend went backstage and put on the costumes of Pozzo and Lucky. Jerry picked up the whip, put the hat on his head, attached the rope to his friend's neck and shouted, "On! Back! Dance!" *Godot* achieved our purpose: it gave Jerry Johnson a theatrical image, offered him an experience that wouldn't have

Excerpted from an interview which appeared in the *Tulane Drama Review*, Vol. IX, No. 4, T28, Summer 1965, copyright © 1965 by the *Tulane Drama Review*. Reprinted by permission. The participants in the interview were Richard Schechner, Gil Moses, John O'Neal, Murray Levy, and Denise Nicholas.

been there but for us. This kid had something he could use, play with, think with, live with.

SCHECHNER: This raises a question. I've seen the FST *Godot* in New Orleans, McComb, and New York. The FST isn't one theater, it's three. The audiences don't come together. At the New School in New York people came to do their Movement duty; we helped them cope with their hangups and they gave us money. In New Orleans people had alternative choices those nights and they chose to come to the FST. Speaking to them afterward, I knew they'd enjoyed the shows and wanted to see more. In McComb the audience was fascinated by a new experience. It wasn't a "meeting," and it wasn't a movie: it was something else. Someone opened the window. But these audiences contradict each other. Can you play for them all in the same way? What about the risk of patronizing?

LEVY: If you are legitimately trying to open avenues of communication—regardless of motives—you are not patronizing. As an actor in *Godot* I was trying to open up communications in New York, I was trying to shock an audience I disliked—I already disliked it when I worked there before joining the FST —and that I feel comes to every theater with the wrong attitude; they're as dead as the theater they see. But in the south the experience isn't sterile.

O'NEAL: Which is to say that the contradictions exist. The audiences demand different things.

MOSES: Within the framework of the play all the audience asks for is good acting. . . .

O'NEAL: No. Murray is right: the way he feels demands certain things of him as an actor—he plays Gogo differently. He never blew his nose at an audience anywhere but in New York, he never kicked his clothes at them. But these things become contradictions only when you're not certain of your stand or where you stand; then you're subject to the mirror an audience brings you. You oscillate more when you're uncertain of what assertions you want to make.

SCHECHNER: I was struck by something else watching the three audiences. The New York audience looked for meanings; they saw the play in the context of a hundred critics. In New Orleans and in McComb they looked at Beckett's play—right in the face—and they laughed at the characters. "We're *not* waiting!" they said, during and after the play. These audiences weren't waiting for Godot like Gogo and Didi; built right into the text of the play was an alienation and the audiences stood back and looked at these silly characters. Maybe it was all a delusion: maybe they really were waiting but didn't realize it. Still, it was not a play of despair in Mississippi. But New York is a rich enough city for despair to become an occupation.

MOSES: The problems are the same in McComb and New York: neither audience accepts itself as waiting. But the New York audience is intellectually better able to deal with the meaning of the play; they scratch their heads and ask, "What's the meaning of this despair?" Because of the academic approach, they usually miss the play. But in McComb they don't miss seeing and enjoying the play because of preconceived notions. They come to the play with ideas only about what amuses them, but theater can expand that idea.

SCHECHNER: The McComb audience doesn't have the kind of despair which depends upon the separation of thought and act. *Godot* was really a comedy in New Orleans and Mississippi. They laughed at Lucky; in New York they were embarrassed by a Negro at the end of a white man's rope.

MOSES: O.K. In Mississippi they sat *outside* of the play, maybe not following the verbal gymnastics but getting the theatrical images which burn in their brains.

SCHECHNER: But why did you put on whiteface halfway through the tour? For me that destroyed the reality of the play.

MOSES: James Cromwell, who directed it, could answer that better than I. The reason was, I think, that the audience couldn't go beyond the Pozzo and Lucky situation: the image of the white man holding the rope around a Negro's neck shocked them out of comprehension.

NICHOLAS: Whiteface immediately stopped that first black-white reaction and forced the audience to deal with something else. Maybe they don't know what this "something else" is until the end of the play or until they get home. But in the discussions—after we began using whiteface—it was clear that the change worked with the audience. It brought them closer to the human heart of the play.

SCHECHNER: The problem for me was that the whiteface robbed *Godot* of reality; we no longer were on a country road. It made the production phony.

O'NEAL: Finally we rejected the idea of whiteface, but kept it anyway because there was no other way to deal with the problem of racial hangups. My feeling is that we should accept these hangups and deal with them—with whatever is implicit in the play—and try to manipulate it from that point of view. No matter how you handle it there are going to be connotations. We had a white Gogo and a Negro Didi; two Negroes doing the roles would have been different, etc. But that's implicit in our milieu. Cromwell didn't agree with that because he couldn't accept the milieu. If we keep *Godot* in the repertory—and we will—we'll have to work these things out.

GODOT AT SAN QUENTIN

MARTIN ESSLIN

On November 19, 1957, a group of worried actors were preparing to face their audience. The actors were members of the company of the San Francisco Actors' Workshop. The audience consisted of fourteen hundred convicts at the San Quentin penitentiary. No live play had been performed at San Quentin since Sarah Bernhardt appeared there in 1913. Now, forty-four years later, the play that had been chosen, largely because no woman appeared in it, was Samuel Beckett's *Waiting for Godot*.

No wonder the actors and Herbert Blau, the director, were apprehensive. How were they to face one of the toughest audiences in the world with a highly obscure, intellectual play that had produced near riots among a good many highly sophisticated audiences in Western Europe? Herbert Blau decided to prepare the San Quentin audience for what was to come. He stepped onto the stage and addressed the packed, darkened North Dining Hall—a sea of flickering matches that the convicts tossed over their shoulders after lighting their cigarettes. Blau compared the play to a piece of jazz music "to which one must listen for whatever one may find in it." In the same way, he hoped, there would be some meaning, some personal significance for each member of the audience in *Waiting for Godot*.

The curtain parted. The play began. And what had bewildered the sophisticated audiences of Paris, London, and New York was immediately grasped by an audience of convicts. As the writer of "Memoirs of a First-Nighter" put it in the columns of the prison paper, the *San Quentin News*:

From *The Theatre of the Absurd* (New York: Doubleday & Company, 1961), copyright © 1961 by Martin Esslin. Reprinted by permission of the publisher. Quotations from the *San Quentin News* by kind permission of the librarian.

The trio of muscle-men, biceps overflowing, who parked all 642 lbs on the aisle and waited for the girls and funny stuff. When this didn't appear they audibly fumed and audibly decided to wait until the house lights dimmed before escaping. They made one error. They listened and looked two minutes too long—and stayed. Left at the end.

Or as the writer of the lead story of the same paper reported, under the headline, "San Francisco Group Leaves S. Q. Audience Waiting for Godot":

From the moment Robin Wagner's thoughtful and limbo-like set was dressed with light, until the last futile and expectant handclasp was hesitantly activated between the two searching vagrants, the San Francisco company had its audience of captives in its collective hand. . . . Those that had felt a less controversial vehicle should be attempted as a first play here had their fears allayed a short five minutes after the Samuel Beckett piece began to unfold.

A reporter from the San Francisco *Chronicle* who was present noted that the convicts did not find it difficult to understand the play. One prisoner told him, "Godot is society." Said another: "He's the outside." A teacher at the prison was quoted as saying, "They know what is meant by waiting . . . and they knew if Godot finally came, he would only be a disappointment." The leading article of the prison paper showed how clearly the writer had understood the meaning of the play:

It was an expression, symbolic in order to avoid all personal error, by an author who expected each member of his audience to draw his own conclusions, making his own errors. It asked nothing in point, it forced no dramatized moral on the viewer, it held out no specific hope. . . . We're still waiting for Godot, and shall continue to wait. When the scenery gets too drab and the action too slow, we'll call each other names *and swear to part forever—but then, there's no place to go!*

It is said that Godot himself, as well as turns of phrase and characters from the play, have since become a permanent part of the private language, the institutional mythology of San Quentin.

Beckett knew instinctively that *Mercier et Camier* was but an experimental approximation to what he was trying to achieve. Hence his refusal to publish it and his complete lack of interest in it. His refusal must be respected, of course, and I reproduce here—with his kind permission—no more than is necessary for the genetic study of *Godot*.

When I told Mr. Beckett that I was struck by the similarities between the two works and that, to put it crudely, they seemed to have come out of the same stable, his only comment was to the effect that he could remember nothing about *Mercier et Camier* ("a dreadful book"), and had cast it completely out of his mind. Seeing that it was written in 1945, four years before *Godot* (with *Molloy, Eleutheria,* and *Malone meurt* in between), it is quite credible that a writer with a headful of dying worlds crying out to be drawn into existence should drive an unwanted embryo from his conscious mind. But any work of art, once it has been created, never leaves its author intact, whatever he might think of it. As Dr. Fletcher points out, for example, Part II of *Molloy* derives from *Mercier et Camier* and in places follows it quite closely.[2] The resemblances between *Mercier et Camier* and *Godot* are of quite a different order, however. That they are unconscious similarities one need have no doubt, but they are none the less highly informative and, together with the manuscript of *En attendant Godot*, throw some new light upon the question of the making of *Godot*.[3]

There are many coincidences of style and theme in *Mercier et Camier* and *Godot*. Particular attention will be paid to the

[2] John Fletcher, *The Novels of Samuel Beckett* (London: Chatto and Windus, 1964), p. 129.

[3] The manuscript of *En attendant Godot*, which Mr. Beckett kindly allowed me to read, thus making this study possible, consists of an exercise book measuring 8½ x 7 inches. Beckett wrote on each right-hand page to the end of the book, then continued on each left-hand page beginning at the beginning of the book again. He told me that there were several typescript versions between the manuscript and the first edition. The second edition (also 1952) contains minor textual changes, and constitutes the definitive edition upon which the present text is based.

most interesting points illuminated by the unpublished docu-
ments—namely, the setting of the play; the origins and meaning of the tree; Godot; the rendezvous and the theme of waiting; the creation of the characters and the relationships between
them; the perfection of the dialogue and the suppression of
certain precise details to be found in the manuscript.

The essential difference between *Mercier et Camier* and
Godot is that the two old men in the novel are completely
disponibles, able to wander aimlessly on their vague quest,
whereas the two tramps in the play are tied to one spot. This
results in radical dissimilarities in structure. Mercier and
Camier dissipate their energies in the search for divers objects
—their bag, their umbrella, their bicycle—as well as for the
ultimate unspecified thing or person motivating their wander-
ings. In *Godot* all this is streamlined, as all the hopes of
Vladimir and Estragon are concentrated upon one objective:
the meeting with Godot, with whom a rendezvous has been
arranged. Vladimir and Estragon do, in fact, go away from the
meeting place at night, and they lose sight of each other during
the action of the play, greeting each other like long-lost friends
a few moments later. Similarly the journey of Mercier and
Camier is punctuated by regular returns *chez* Hélène (a singularly accommodating acquaintance). The center of interest in
the novel is in the time spent away from "base"; in the play,
the center is in the returning and the waiting. The importance
of waiting and meeting is a notable feature of the novel too,
together with the questing theme which Beckett took up again
in *Molloy*.

Mercier and Camier arrange to meet at a place called le
Square Saint-Ruth. . . . [They] miss each other several times
at the rendezvous, but eventually both arrive at the spot at the
same moment:

> *Leur joie fut donc pendant un instant extrême, celle de
> Mercier et celle de Camier, lorsqu'après cinq et dix minutes
> respectivement d'inquiète musardise, débouchant simultané-*

ment sur la place, *ils se trouvèrent face à face, pour la pre-mière fois depuis la veille au soir.*

The similarity of situation and emotion with that of the beginning of Act II of *Godot* is striking:

Ils se regardent longuement, en reculant, avançant, et penchant la tête comme devant un objet d'art, tremblant de plus en plus l'un vers l'autre, puis soudain s'étreignent, en se tapant sur le dos. [p. 50]

So strong is the theme of joyful reunion that Beckett returns to it very much later in *Mercier et Camier*:

Ta main, dit Camier, tes deux mains.
Pour quoi faire? dit Mercier.
Pour les serrer dans les miennes, dit Camier.
Les mains se cherchèrent sous la table, parmi les jambes, se trouvèrent, se serrèrent, une petite entre deux grandes, une grande entre deux petites.
Je nous aurais bien proposé de nous embrasser, dit Mercier, il y a si longtemps que nous ne nous sommes pas embrassés, mais j'ai peur des représailles.

In Act II of *Godot*, Vladimir and Estragon make up after quarreling:

—*Ta main!*
—*La voilà!*
—*Viens dans mes bras!*
—*Tes bras?*
—*(ouvrant les bras) Là-dedans!*
—*Allons-y. (Ils s'embrassent.)* [p. 67]

Mercier and Camier wait in a public shelter for the rain to stop. Their conversation has the same qualities as that of their two counterparts in *Godot*; it is that of two people forced into passive waiting by something beyond their control. The "agent complaisant de la malignité universelle" which forces them to wait is in this case nothing more mysterious than the rain; the strong term applied to it might seem more appropriate to Godot.

Mercier and his companion argue about who kept whom waiting. Camier replies, "On n'attend ni ne fait attendre qu'à partir d'un moment convenu d'avance."

This statement is the very core of *Godot*. The very fact that Vladimir and Estragon are waiting presupposes that a time was fixed. In the manuscript of the play this arrangement is not just verbal, as in the published text [p. 9], but *written down by Godot himself*:

> —*Tu es sûr que c'était ce soir?*
> —*Quoi?*
> —*Notre rendez-vous.*
> —*Diable!* (Il cherche dans ses poches.) *Il l'a écrit.*
> [He pulls out a number of pieces of paper and hands one over.] *Qu'est-ce que tu lis?*
> —*"Samedi soir et suivants." Quelle façon de s'exprimer!*
> —*Tu vois!*
> —*(rendant le papier) Mais sommes-nous samedi?*

For Godot to have written the words himself, he must have a physical reality; this obvious consequence led to the omission of the piece of paper. But we see from this first version something not entirely without significance, that Beckett originally envisaged the two characters to be waiting for a real reason.

We see in *Mercier et Camier* the seeds of doubt about the precise nature of the arrangement to meet. Camier concludes, "Nous ne saurons jamais à quelle heure nous nous sommes donné rendez-vous, aujourd'hui. Ne cherchons donc plus." The importance which Mercier and Camier attach to this matter is curious, since in their case it is in fact a very trivial point. Only when it was later transferred to the cosmic situation of

Vladimir and Estragon did it assume its full latent significance. . . .

The manuscript reveals that none of the characters are in-
dividualized to the extent of having names when they first
appear on the written page—proof enough that it is the original
draft. The opening stage direction reads, "Un vieillard assis" . . .
"Entre un deuxième vieillard, *ressemblant au premier*" [my
italics]. Differentiation between them only gradually crystal-
lizes. Vladimir is the first to receive his name. The other
vieillard is called "Lévy" right up to the end of Act I. The
word "Estragon" is written on the back of the last page of Act I,
and he becomes Estragon from that point on.

The first entrance of Pozzo and Lucky reads thus in the
manuscript: "Entrent deux messieurs, un très grand et un
petit." They are then referred to as "le grand" and "le petit."
Pozzo is not given a name until he introduces himself [p. 16]—
which he does in the manuscript with the words "Je m'appelle
Pozzo." Of particular interest is the fact that the reason why
Lucky is so named is clarified by the context in which he first
receives his name. Pozzo is explaining the protocol with regard
to the bones [p. 21]: "Mais en principe les os reviennent au
porteur"—the manuscript reads—". . . à Lucky"; that is to
say, he is lucky *because he gets the bones.* Just to keep the spirit
of contradiction alive, however, it must be stressed that this is
not the only "official" explanation. Mr. Beckett's verbal reply
to my question, "Is Lucky so named because he has found his
Godot?" was: "I suppose he is Lucky to have no more expectations." . . .

The most human quality of the two tramps is the ambivalence of their feelings for each other. They want to be independent but dread being parted. They pretend to get on
famously alone, but know they are destined to remain together.
These contradictory emotions govern the relationships between
Mercier and Camier also. . . .

Dependence has a slight edge over independence for the two
characters in the novel:

Certes il fallait de la force pour rester avec Camier, comme il en fallait pour rester avec Mercier, mais moins qu'il n'en fallait pour la bataille du soliloque.

And yet for Camier, the possibility of separation is always there, sometimes as a threat to the slightly less self-reliant Mercier:

> *. . . je me demande souvent, assez souvent, si nous ne ferions pas mieux de nous quitter sans plus tarder.*
> *Tu ne m'auras pas par les sentiments, dit Mercier.*

This is clearly echoed in *Godot* [p. 54], when Estragon suggests, "On ferait mieux de se séparer."

The fatality of Mercier and Camier's "togetherness" is epitomized in words which are more applicable to Vladimir and Estragon, since Mercier and Camier do, in fact, part and cease to know each other (or pretend to):

> *Les voilà donc sur la route, sensiblement rafraîchis quand même, et chacun sait l'autre proche, le sent, le croit, le craint, l'espère, le nie et n'y peut rien.*

Estragon's crowning, pathetic appeal for confirmation of their ability to get on together ("On ne se débrouille p~~ ~~ mal, hein, Didi, tous les deux ensemble?"—p. 61) has its counterpart when Camier remarks:

> *Il y a des fois où c'est un véritable plaisir de causer avec toi. Je ne suis pas méchant, au fond, dit Mercier.*

The fraternity of the two couples, so mysteriously destroyed at the end of the novel (whereas it just as mysteriously avoids destruction at the end of both acts of the play, thus becoming one of its major themes) is a very important element of their common origin; Vladimir looks after Estragon, feeds him, protects him, and Camier plays the same role. He makes

Mercier eat—much against his will, since he has sunk into a
state of nauseated depression during Camier's absence.

Je me demandais si tu allais revenir . . .
    *Mercier réfléchit un instant. Il faut être Camier pour ne
pas abandonner Mercier, dit-il.*

Camier does not simply become Vladimir, however. He is the
more sceptical of the two, and this equates him more with
Estragon. The manuscript of *Godot* is more self-consistent than
the final text in regard to Vladimir's intelligence; when Vladimir and Estragon contemplate hanging themselves from the
tree [p. 11], Estragon has to explain why they cannot both do
it. The manuscript reads:

VLADIMIR: *Je ne comprends pas.*
LÉVY: *Mais . . . voyons. Ça marcherait avec moi. Ça pourrait
    très bien ne pas marcher avec toi.*
VLADIMIR: *Je n'avais pas pensé à ça.*
LÉVY: *Qui peut le plus peut le moins.*
VLADIMIR: *Attendons voir ce qu'il va nous dire.*

There is no condescending pigeon-English, and the oblique
reference to the thieves on the Cross ("Il y a une chance sur
deux") is thus shown to be an afterthought. However, the
point is that there is a slight discrepancy in the final text, since
it is Vladimir who seizes Pozzo's meaning first [p. 32] when he
asks how his little speech went ("Bon? Moyen?", etc.). The
manuscript reads differently:

LÉVY (comprenant): *Oh très bien, tout à fait bien.*
VLADIMIR: *Oh très très bien, très très très bien.*

There is no comic *accent anglais.*
    The manuscript makes Estragon (Lévy) alone guess the
name of Lucky's dance. He suggests simply "La mort du

canard"—all the obscene and symbolic overtones of the final version are later elaborations. . . .

Estragon's need for food, satisfied minimally by the raw vegetables offered by Vladimir, has its counterpart in Mercier, who is dissatisfied when Camier returns with the wrong kind of cake. The gradual deterioration in food is common to play and novel ("Hier des gâteaux, aujourd'hui des sandwichs, demain du pain sec et jeudi des pierres" is the way the situation is summed up in the novel); this reminds us that in *Godot* Beckett has taken the men to the absolute extreme of destitution. They begin and end just this side of the stones.

There are a number of similar exchanges in the novel and the play which it would be tedious to quote in full. The "after you—no, after you" routine [p. 67], the frequent references to the thief who was saved (a recurrent theme throughout Beckett's works), the compulsive talking to fill the void [p. 54], the self-awareness and self-depreciation [*passim*]. The comedy extracted from the subject of suicide is subtly caught in the novel too:

> *Où allons-nous de ce pas mal assuré? dit Camier.*
> *Nous nous dirigeons je crois vers le canal, dit Mercier.*
> *Déjà? dit Camier.*

Pozzo's disquisition on the horrors of night [p. 31] is foreshadowed in three quite separate parts of the novel, and yet there is no repetition of words; this is an important point in comparing the two works as a whole, for while much of the dialogue in *Mercier et Camier* consists of short, sharp, pithy exchanges in a style strongly resembling that of *Godot*, and while there is the same need to make conversation out of nothing—for example, on the subject of whether to open an umbrella when it is pouring with rain or wait until the sun is hot and then use it as a sunshade—very little of the actual dialogue of the novel is repeated in the play.

The dialogue of *Godot* is a great improvement on that of *Mercier et Camier*. The manuscript of *Godot* shows that

Beckett has an infallible ear for what to cut. In Act II, for
example, there were originally about ten additional pages of
dialogue inserted between p. 66 and p. 68 of the final French
text. They contain an argument (of which the "Oh pardon"
routine is the essence) elaborately built round the question
"Est-ce que c'est la peine?" This question takes them ten pages
to formulate, just as it takes them many pages to ask Pozzo why
Lucky does not put down his bags. Beckett rightly saw the
danger of tedium and repeated effect here—although it would
have stood in a novel, as it is a true *tour de force*.

Another example occurs on p. 36 of the final text of *Godot*.
Between the juxtaposed words "Enchaînez" and "Assez" the
following originally appeared:

POZZO: *Ou bien il ne fait rien.*
LÉVY: *Le salaud.*
VLADIMIR: *Et quand vous ne lui demandez rien?*
POZZO: *Ça ne change rien.*
LÉVY: *Il fait ce qu'il veut.*
VLADIMIR: *Quand il veut.*
LÉVY: *Comme il veut.*
VLADIMIR: *Que vous lui demandiez ou non.*
POZZO: *Plus ou moins.*
LÉVY: *Et quand vous lui demandez de s'arrêter?*
POZZO: *Ça ne change rien.*
LÉVY: *Il ne s'arrête pas.*
POZZO: *Quelquefois.*
VLADIMIR: *Mais pas toujours.*
POZZO: *Non.*
LÉVY: *Et il a toujours été comme ça?*
POZZO: *Non.*
VLADIMIR: *Depuis quand?*
POZZO: *Je ne sais pas.*
LÉVY: *Assez.*

This long quotation is given because it is instructive. It shows
how miraculously the final text of *Godot* manages to avoid the

tedium of this suppressed page even though the intellectual substance of much of the play is no greater than this. The danger of taking the quality of the dialogue for granted, of failing to appreciate the manipulation of language and the flow of words, is diminished by the realization that a lesser writer would have finished with a book full of passages like the suppressed one quoted, no doubt congratulating himself on creating the Theater of Inaction in a massive prefatory note.

It is for similar reasons that Beckett has declined to publish *Mercier et Camier*, with its frequently cyclic, hair-splitting dialogue tediously dependent upon forgetfulness of what has just been said or decided. These features are to be found in *Godot* as well, but used with great discretion, with an eye and an ear for the shape of sentence, exchange, scene, act, and total structure.

Mercier et Camier illuminates the situation of the characters in *Godot* by showing that Beckett does not push them to the extreme suffering of self-aware solitude. Those who think *Godot* depressingly morbid, exploiting *ad nauseam* the basic misery of a godless universe, would realize on reading the novel that the hours or days of anguish on the *haute lande*, when the narrative becomes turgid and incoherent, mark the mysterious transformation of the *pseudocouple* Mercier/Camier into the *pseudocouple* Vladimir/Estragon. They become imbued with a totally different quality. Whereas Mercier and Camier rarely rise above the level of two rather dirty old men, Didi and Gogo positively *glow* by comparison; their condition is so infused with timeless, tragic quality that it acquires a density and depth quite lacking in the novel.

SEVEN NOTES ON *WAITING FOR GODOT*

ALFONSO SASTRE

1. Of Realism and Its Forms

Waiting for Godot is a fantastic drama for some people who find it curious, obscure, distant, arbitrary, strange, capricious, withdrawn from reality. Perhaps a posthumous secretion of "surrealism." Perhaps an obscure illustration of a preposterous philosophy of existence. Perhaps the pure representation of delirium. For these spectators, then, the drama has nothing to do with their life, with their daily bus ride, their office routine, or their conversations.

For them, *Waiting for Godot* is like a strange theatrical animal; like the dramatization of some oneiric context or of a magical experience. For others, we are before something even worse: a hallucination, a work conceived through the decay of a sick mind, or perhaps the joke of an author who tried to shock simple people. . . .

This attitude toward *Waiting for Godot* is incomprehensible to me, since I have never seen a more realistic drama; to say it another way, I have never seen a less fantastic work. . . . The term "realism" is normally used to designate one of its forms: the form which we might call "naturalist"; the form fostered by Antoine for the Théâtre Libre; superficial realism; photographic testimony. But this does not exhaust the meaning of the term. I have pointed out elsewhere the existence of a deepening impulse which has made possible the complex forms of deepened realism in the literature and art of our time. This process is nourished, in great part, by techniques developed by esthetic movements with anti-realistic aims. All these movements—"isms"—have been fertile for realism. The ultimate result of

From *Primer Acto*, No. 1 (April, 1957). Translated from the Spanish "Siete Notas sobre 'Esperando A Godot'" by Leonard C. Pronko, copyright © 1966 by Leonard C. Pronko. Reprinted by permission of Literary Discoveries Inc.

these experiments is the incorporation of their most valuable precipitates into the principal adventure of art, its fundamental line of development: realism. . . .

What I meant when I said that *Waiting for Godot* is a realistic drama is this: that it is a work situated in the main line of development of the history of the theater; nourished, of course, through foreign experiments—many of them with anti-realistic intentions—which have helped to enrich the author's methods of capturing reality. The richness of these methods makes Beckett's picture seem strange to some eyes, just as the radiograph of his lungs may look strange, unrecognizable, to a man with bad lungs. Nevertheless, *this* is the most profound reality of his anatomophysiology, rather than that smiling and complacent photograph which he exhibits on his identity card. . . .

2. The Great Circus of the World

Beckett discovers the circus as an existential representation. This pair, the "clown" and the "augustus," is a simplified presentation of a complex relationship: that of man and his fellow. The "clown" and the "augustus" are two men who do not understand each other. Because of this, we laugh. Because of this, we might also cry. (Some children—let us remember—weep at the sight of circus slaps and blows.) In spite of all the love which the clowns feel for one another, they are brutally separated, as though they belonged to two different biological species. On the one hand, that flour-white face, that large painted eyebrow, that spangled costume, those white stockings, that average mentality. On the other, a huge nose, an immense mouth, vast clown pants, an alarm clock in the pocket, great shoes, and an incredible mentality. Everything is prepared so that they will not understand one another. They will make grotesque efforts, they will slap each other, play musical instruments, perform the most incredible pirouettes in order to express themselves. They will not succeed in understanding each other.

Beckett takes his point of departure from this circus pair. He destroys their external differences. He rubs out the huge eye-brow. Takes off the big nose. Erases the bright colors. Washes off the make-up, so that the true sunken eyes appear. He throws the pair into the circus ring. They are flung down. They wait. They get bored. They play.

We laugh, but our laughter rings hollow. What has happened? We have recognized ourselves.

3. At Last, a Tragicomedy

With *Waiting for Godot*, the history of the theater at last has a pure tragicomedy, which breaks with classical tragicomedy. *Waiting for Godot* stands for a great rupture and the possibility of revolutionary change. . . . Whether the provisional tag "avant-garde" will become permanently attached to this work, depends upon whether the path of pure tragicomedy is continued. (There are already signs of this eruption of pure tragicomedy on the contemporary theatrical horizon, and the present "avant-garde" theater of Paris bears this tragicomic mark.)

The phenomenon may be important. Classical tragicomedy in the Spanish style—which was revolutionary insofar as it tended to destroy the Greco-Roman fetish of tragedy and comedy as separate and incommunicable forms—may be superseded by tragicomedy as a third distinct genre, that is to say, tragicomedy as a drama based upon a situation which is characteristic and different from the tragic or the comic situation.

Classical tragicomedy—with which we are still living—was conceived according to an alternation of comic and tragic situations. Upon a basic line (which was usually tragic) there appeared comic variations, usually introduced by the "gracioso," the buffoon. This was called tragicomedy. At other times, upon a basic comic line there appeared fleetingly tragic variations. This was also called tragicomedy.

The pure tragicomic situation had to be established in the theater; and it is now being established: that mysterious situation before which, horrified, we laugh.

We laugh, but we are paralyzed with horror. We laugh, but

our eyes are wet. Chaplin made this part of cinema art, and it had already been invented in the theater. (The "grotesque tragedies" of Carlos Arniches were, or might have been, just this.) And this is what *Waiting for Godot* establishes gloriously upon the stage.

4. A Death Certificate for Hope

Waiting for Godot has something about it of crepuscular lament, of a posthumous will and testament, of the forerunner of the end, of a letter of last reprieve, a cry for help in the night, a funeral chant. *Waiting for Godot* is a death certificate for hope. We will keep on coming to the appointment, beneath the tree which is one day skeletal and the next in bloom. We will continue killing our desperate boredom with games, words, hunger, ideas of suicide. But we already know that Godot will not show up. We will continue waiting, but our waiting will now be a wait without hope; a hopeless hope.

Waiting for Godot seems a posthumous work. We are in the presence of a bottle left by a shipwrecked sailor. We read this desperate declaration, but the man who signed it is drowned in the sea. Before his last breath, we see that he witnessed horrible scenes; that the men, before sinking into final sleep, devoured one another. (What is the Pozzo-Lucky relationship, but a cannibalistic one?) The drama is a message found in a bottle. A creature from the raft of the Medusa has spoken before dying. The reader of the message looks out to sea, and perceives no living being; only the sad remains of a frightful shipwreck.

We now know that cannibalism and blasphemy are the terrible signs of being abandoned. We know that the men have tried everything before taking the leap into nothingness, before falling from the viaduct, before the last imprecations. . . .

The certificate of death—or the epitaph—of Estragon and Vladimir might say: "The afternoon they died they were sad. They had come to the appointment as usual, near a tree, and they felt more alone than ever. A chilly wind was blowing, and no one came. They did not know whether it was there, but they had no other place in which to wait. They looked at each other a moment and wept sadly, with helplessness which was the summing up of their existence. They separated forever. They died—each one alone—of cold and of being abandoned. They cried out before dying. And then the world remained alone."

5. "Being Rent Asunder"

During the preparation of these notes I asked myself what was the ultimate and most profound reason for the fear—if I laughed, I did so fearfully—roused in me by this drama. And I told myself, in manner of explanation, that *Waiting for Godot* is above all a strangely lucid dramatic representation of the rending apart of the human being. That is the ultimate ontological basis of *Waiting for Godot*. The human being is nothing more than bloody, broken shreds and patches. This business of the "analogy" of being is nothing more than the sophistry of logic to cover up the tearing apart, to hide the wound, to lessen the hemorrhage. But the human being continues to lose blood, and we witness this horrible bleeding. The beings grow pale because they need one another, and they do not succeed in communicating. They send out an S O S. No one answers. Neither Godot, nor his fellow man....

There is at times a kind of nostalgia for the days when the rending apart had not yet taken place, when the Other had not yet appeared. It is like nostalgia for a paradise. But they inevitably return to the pitilessness of being rent asunder. . . .

Waiting for Godot is above all the spectacle of pitilessness, of lack of solidarity, of the rending asunder of being.

6. Toward a Metaphysics of Boredom

It seems that Casiano—in the fifth century of our era—was the first person to realize that one could be bored. He observed the boredom—the "sourness"—of the monks, and described it in order to combat it. It was like a sickness or a sin. The monks felt a "horror loci," a boredom of their cell, and, anguished, gazed at the horizon through their windows. From Casiano until our day boredom has concerned people. It has been named as the principle of all things—Kierkegaard—through which being in its totality is revealed to us—Heidegger. Its psychological mechanism has been studied. It has been the object of literary and cinematographic representation; we have witnessed boredom as it exists in specific forms of life—Fellini, boredom of the provincial town; Bardem, boredom of the Saturday afternoon; *Marty*, Sunday boredom, etc. We have seen how in boredom everything loses its meaning, and we may even go so far as to commit a gratuitous crime. In literature and in the theater we have been shown mechanical games—Saroyan's *Time of Your Life*, Adamov's *Ping Pong*, etc.,—card games, solitary games, billiard tables. Time and again, we have seen the personal and collective boredom of the characters, and their defense mechanisms, from the purely personal mechanism of dipsomania, for example, to collective mechanisms—social (parties, etc.) or asocial (hoodlumism). The theme of boredom is not new on the horizon of our culture, but until now perhaps we had no literary work which expressed it in all its existential profundity. The psychological and social levels are transcended here; *Waiting for Godot* is a valuable contribution toward a metaphysics of boredom.

7. A Drama in Which Absolutely Nothing Happens

It has been said of *Waiting for Godot*, with destructive intent, that it is a drama in which absolutely nothing happens. "And does that seem a small accomplishment?" we should ask. This is precisely what is so fascinating about *Waiting for Godot*: that nothing happens. It is a lucid testimony of nothingness. But while we are left cold by many dramas of intrigue in which a great deal happens, this "nothing happens" of *Waiting for Godot* keeps us in suspense. These men who are bored cast us out of our own boredom; their boredom produces our catharsis, and we follow their adventure breathlessly, for they have suddenly placed us before the "nothing happens" of our lives. The gray and meaningless mass of our everyday existence is suddenly illuminated, disclosing its true structure, naked and desolate. That is the great revelation. Besides, we are not before a plotless drama. We are before a mono-situational plot. Considered in this light, *Waiting for Godot* is a drama which conforms to the artistic requirements of traditional drama. It is rooted in sure ground, the only ground in which theater can be seriously rooted: situation. Thus, "nothing happens" can be the form in which the most extraordinary and profound events are presented, just as "many things happen" can be a form of emptiness.

Waiting for Godot captures this "nothing happens" which constitutes our daily existence. For this reason, it is a familiar picture, a radiographic plate in which we recognize ourselves with horror. The story of *Waiting for Godot* is precisely the story of our lives.

LIFE IN THE BOX

HUGH KENNER

The drama is a ritual enacted in an enclosed space into which fifty or more people are staring. They are all more or less patiently waiting for something: the Reversal, the Discovery, the *deus ex machina*, or even the final curtain. Settled numbly for the evening, they accept whatever interim diversions the stage can provide: tramps in bowler hats, for instance.

The space into which they are staring is characterized in some way: for instance, A *country road. A tree. Evening.* "Evening" means that the illumination on stage is not much brighter than in the auditorium. "A country road" means that there is no set to look at. As for the tree, an apologetic thing tentatively identified as a leafless weeping willow, it serves chiefly to denote the spot, like the intersection (coordinates O,O) of the Cartesian axes. "You're sure it was here?" "What?" "That we were to wait." "He said by the tree." If it accretes meaning of an anomalous sort in the course of the evening, reminding us, when the two tramps stand beneath it with a rope, of ampler beams which once suspended the Savior and two thieves, or again of the fatal tree in Eden (and the garden has, sure enough, vanished), or even of the flowering staff in *Tannhäuser*, it does this not by being explicated but simply by its insistent continual presence, during which, as adjacent events diffract the bleak light, we begin to entertain mild hallucinations about it. Only in a theater can we be made to look at a mock tree for that length of time. Drama is distinguished from all other forms of art by its control over the *time* spent by the spectator in the presence of its significant elements.

These events, these elements, assert only their own nagging existence. "The theatrical character," remarked Alain Robbe-Grillet in this connection, "*is on stage*, this is his primary quality—he is there." Hence, "the essential function of the theatrical performance: to show what this fact of *being there* consists of." Or as Beckett was later to write of a later play, "Hamm as stated, and Clov as stated, together as stated, *nec tecum nec sine te*, in such a place, and in such a world, that's all I can manage, more than I could."

In *Waiting for Godot*, the place with its tree is stated, together with a single actor engaged in a mime with his boot. His inability to get it off is the referent of his first words, "Nothing to be done," a sentence generally reserved for more portentous matters. To him enter the second actor, as in the medial phase of Greek Theater, and their talk commences. What they talk about first is the fact that they are both there, the one fact that is demonstrably true not only in art's agreed world but before our eyes. It is even the one certainty that survives an evening's waiting:

BOY: *What am I to tell Mr. Godot, sir?*
VLADIMIR: *Tell him* . . . (he hesitates) . . . *tell him you saw
us.* (Pause.) *You did see us, didn't you?*
BOY: *Yes Sir.*

[p. 34a]

The realities stated with such insistence are disquietingly
provisional. The tree is plainly a sham, and the two tramps
are simply filling up time until a proper dramatic entertainment
can get under way. They are helping the management fulfill, in
a minimal way, its contract with the ticket holders. The resources of vaudeville are at their somewhat incompetent dis-
posal: bashed hats, dropped pants, tight boots, the kick, the
pratfall, the improper story. It will suffice if they can stave off
a mass exodus until Godot comes, in whom we are all so
interested. Beckett, it is clear, has cunningly doubled his play
with that absence of a play which every confirmed theatergoer
has at some time or other experienced, the advertized cynosure
having missed a train or overslept or indulged in temperament.
The tramps have plainly not learned parts; they repeatedly
discuss what to do next ("What about hanging ourselves?")
and observe from time to time that tedium is accumulating
[as on pp. 23a and b]. Thus a non-play comments on itself. Or
the audience of the non-play is reminded that others the previous night sat in these seats witnessing the identical futility
("What did we do yesterday?" "In my opinion we were here.")
and that others in turn will sit there watching on successive
nights for an indeterminate period.

—We'll come back to-morrow [*says tramp No. 1*].
—And then the day after to-morrow.
—Possibly.
—And so on.

[p. 10b]

And so on, until the run of the production ends. It will end,
presumably, when there are no longer spectators interested,
though it is difficult to explain on Shakespearean premises what

it is that they can be expected to be interested in. Or perhaps not so difficult. What brings the groundlings to *Macbeth?* Why, they are waiting for the severed head. And to *Hamlet?* They are waiting for Garrick (or Irving, or Olivier). And here?

> —Let's go.
> —We can't.
> —Why not?
> —We're waiting for Godot.
> —(despairingly) Ah!   [p. 31b–32a]

The French text manages an inclusiveness denied to English idiom: "Pourquoi?" "On attend Godot." Not "*nous*" but "*on*": Didi, Gogo, and audience alike.

If the seeming improvisation of the tramps denies theatricality, it affirms at the same time quintessential theater, postulating nothing but what we can see on stage: a place, and men present in it, doing what they are doing. And into this quintessential theater there irrupts before long the strident unreality we crave:

> POZZO: (terrifying voice). *I am Pozzo!* (Silence.) *Pozzo!* (Silence.) *Does that name mean nothing to you?* (Silence.) *I say does that name mean nothing to you?*   [p. 15b]

This is at last the veritable stuff, that for which we paid our admissions: an actor, patently, with gestures and grimaces, who has furthermore memorized and rehearsed his part and knows how they talk in plays. He makes his entrance like Tamburlaine driving the pampered jades of Asia (represented, in this low-budget production, by one extra); he takes pains with his elocution, assisted by a vaporizer, like an effete *Heldentenor;* he recites a well-conned set speech on the twilight, with "vibrant," "lyrical," and "prosaic" phrases, and contrapuntal assistance from well-schooled hands (two hands lapsing; two hands flung amply apart; one hand raised in admonition; fingers snapped at the climax, to reinforce the word "pop!"). This is theater; the evening is saved. Surely he is Godot?

But he says not; and we are disconcerted to find him fishing for applause, and from the tramps. They are his audience as we are his and theirs. The play, in familiar Beckett fashion, has gotten inside the play. So too when Lucky (who has also memorized his part) recites his set speech on the descent of human certainty into "the great cold the great dark" ("for reasons unknown but time will tell"), it is for the amusement of his master, and of the tramps, and incidentally of ourselves. The same is true of his symbolic dance, a thing of constrained gestures, as in Nō drama. So the perspective continues to diminish, box within box. In this theater, the tramps. Within their futile world, the finished theatricality of Pozzo. At Pozzo's command, Lucky's speech; within this speech, scholarship, man *in posse* and *in esse*, all that which, officially endorsed, we think we know, notably the labors of the Acacacacademy of Anthropopopometry; within these in turn, *caca* (Fr. colloq., excrement) and *popo*, a chamberpot: a diminution, a delirium.

Such metaphysics as the Beckett theater will permit is entailed in this hierarchy of watchers and watched. Throughout, and notably during Lucky's holocaust of phrases, we clutch at straws of meaning, persuaded at bottom only of one thing, that all four men exist, embodied, gravid, speaking; moving before us, their shadows cast on the wall, their voices echoing in the auditorium, their feet heavy on the boards.

The second act opens with the song about the dog's epitaph, another infinitely converging series of acts and agents. The Unnamable also meditates on this jingle, and discovers its principle: "third verse, as the first, fourth, as the second, fifth, as the third, give us time, give us time and we'll be a multitude"; for it generates an infinite series of unreal beings, epitaph within epitaph within epitaph. Correspondingly, near the end of the act Didi muses over the sleeping Gogo:

At me too someone is looking, of me too someone is saying, *He is sleeping, he knows nothing, let him sleep on.*   [p. 58b]

So we watch Didi move through his part, as he watches Gogo, and meanwhile Lucky's God with the white beard, outside time, without extension, is loving us dearly "with some exceptions for reasons unknown but time will tell."

It remains to recall that the Beckett universe, wherever we encounter it, consists of a shambles of phenomena within which certain symmetries and recurrences are observable, like the physical world as interpreted by early man. So this stage world has its structure and landmarks. We observe, for example, that bowler hats are apparently *de rigueur*, and that they are removed for thinking but replaced for speaking. We observe that moonrise and sunset occur in conjunction two nights running, for this is an ideal cosmology, unless we are to suppose the two acts to be separated by an interval of twenty-nine days. The tree by the same token has budded overnight, like an early miracle. All this is arbitrary because theatrical. Our play draws on Greek theater with its limited number of actors, its crises always off-stage, and its absent divinity; on Nō theater with its symbolic tree, its nuances and its ritual dance; on *commedia dell'arte*, improvised before our eyes; on twentieth-century experimental theater; and on vaudeville with its cast-off clowns, stumblings, shamblings, delicate bawdry, acrobatics, and astringent pointlessness. The final action partakes of the circus repertoire:

> They each take an end of the cord and pull. It breaks. They almost fall.   [p. 60a]

synchronized with a burlesque house misadventure with trousers:

> . . . which, much too big for him, fall about his ankles.
>   [p. 60a]

The student of *Finnegans Wake* will identify this mishap as the play's epiphany,[1] the least learned will note that something

---

[1] Cf. *Finnegans Wake*, p. 508: ". . . I am sorry to have to tell you, hullo and evoe, they were coming down from off him. —How culious an epiphany!"

hitherto invisible has at last been disclosed, and everyone can
agree that the final gesture is to a static propriety:

VLADIMIR: *Pull ON your trousers.*
ESTRAGON: (realizing his trousers are down). *True.*
  He pulls up his trousers.
VLADIMIR: *Well? Shall we go?*
ESTRAGON: *Yes, let's go.*
  They do not move.

Curtain

NOTES FROM THE UNDERGROUND

HERBERT BLAU

For a man who has *chosen* loneliness, there is something
unreal about the theater, a betrayal: the public premises, the
assumption of a contained space, actors, others, an audience. As
though in penance, the drama contracts to a needle's eye. The
action crawls through the eye out of time, "in the dark, in the
dark mud, and a sack—that's all"; or there is "a voice which is
no voice, trying to speak" (I am writing from his conversation),
then the crawling, the mud, "the form of weakness." When you
try to imagine the play before it comes off the printed page, you
may think of Beckett's favorite sculptor Giacometti, whose
figures yield, in metal, as much to the air as the air needs to
surround them.

The true rhythm of Beckett's plays: "I can't, I must." When
the voice rises it can be apocalyptic: "Mene, mene? Naked
bodies. . . . Your light dying! Listen to that! Well, it can die
just as well here, *your* light."

One might say about Beckett in the theater what Walton said about Donne, who slept in his winding sheet but appeared to preach in Saint Paul's when he should have been on his deathbed: "And, when to the amazement of some beholders he appeared in the Pulpit, many of them thought he presented himself not to preach mortification by a living voice: but, mortality by a decayed body and a dying face." Donne, like Beckett, was a man of great erudition. His most searching devotions were born of the Plague. So in *Godot*, the tramps look over the rubble of the audience and say, "A charnel house! A charnel house!" In one little diabolic canter, we have the decay of Western civilization and Beckett's opinion of the modern theater. If, however, the cultural diagnosis seems merely misanthropic, let us go back a few years before *Godot* to another voice, renowned for grandeur and hope: "What is Europe now? It is a rubble-heap, a charnel house, a breeding-ground of pestilence and hate." It is the atmosphere out of which *Godot* was born—the despair, hunger, and disease of postwar Europe— being defined by Winston Churchill.

As Beckett didn't invent despair, neither does he rest in it. Salvation is a fifty-fifty chance ("it's a reasonable percentage"); his favorite parable: the two thieves, one of whom was saved. Because Chance leads Power in the end—Pozzo tied to Lucky —the protective device, the living end, is laughter, "down the snout—Haw!—so. It is the laugh of laughs, the *risus purus*, the laugh laughing at the laugh, the beholding, saluting of the highest joke, in a word the laugh that laughs—silence please, at that which is unhappy." So Nell: "Nothing is funnier than unhappiness, I grant you that. But. . . ." The laughter dies like the funny story told too often. The trick, perhaps, is to find another way of telling it. Technique again, to baffle the fates, and Time. But when technique fails—as it must—more rage. So Hamm: "Use your head, can't you, use your head, you're on earth, there's no cure for that! (*Pause.*) Get out of here and love one another! Lick your neighbor as yourself!"

The message is clear—but the message is not the meaning. As we wade through the boots, the gaffs, the bicycle wheels,

the ubiquitous pipes and spools, the circular dogs, the colossal
trivia and permutations of loss, the spiritual mathematics of his
withered heroes and amputated clowns, you may be bewildered.
But then you accept them as a matter of fact: fact—each
world to its own protocol. For instance: a man needs a hat to
think. "How describe this hat? And why? When my head had
attained I shall not say its definitive but its maximum dimensions, my father said to me, Come, son, we are going to buy
your hat, as though it has pre-existed from time immemorial in
a pre-established place." Where did Lucky's second hat come
from? It was just *there*. In our second production of *Godot*
[San Francisco Actor's Workshop], when Didi and Gogo were
terrified by the invaders who never came, Gogo hid behind the
tree and Didi jumped into a hole we had cut into the front of
the stage. Then, using a technique borrowed from the cowboy
movies, he tossed his hat in the air to test the enemy. No shot,
all clear. One picks up his hat and proceeds. On opening
night, Didi threw his hat into the air. No shot. But nothing
came down. It was perfect. One picks up Lucky's old hat and
proceeds.

For those willing to play the game, the acrostics are alluring,
the virtuosities entrance. But at the end of the wild-goose chase
we are entangled in the net of inexhaustibility. That, rather
than exhaustion, is Beckett's real subject. "You're right," says
Didi, "we're inexhaustible." That, too, is terrifying. It's funny,
but then it's no longer funny. Lest we think the universe too
inscrutable to bear: the hat thrown up by Didi (Ray Fry) had
stuck in the light pipe above. "So much the better, so much the
better." It's the proceeding that counts.

One learns, in doing them, that the plays—with their whoro-
scopic revelations and buried performances—are always looking
in on themselves, throwing up readings, telling you how to do
them. If any dramatist has the right to speak of drama as an
ado about nothing, it is Beckett. And he means what is *there*.
The picture waits to be turned. The window asks to be looked
out of. The tree is meant to be done. The empty landscape
waits to be recognized. The boots wait to be worn. Beckett may

say (at a café in Paris) "that cup, that table, those people—all the same." And yet which of the New Wave—hovering over images with the camera's mind—can invest man-as-object with so much humanity? Why, tree, boot, bowler, and black radish seem more human than the people in other plays.

As for uncertainty of meaning, just perform what he tells you to perform, and you will feel—as if by some equation between doing and feeling—exactly what you need to feel, and in the bones. Climb up the ladder like Clov, backing down the rungs as he must, and you will know why he walks as he does. Speak the speech of Lucky trippingly on the tongue, clutching through all the eschatological gibberish at the loose ends of Western philosophy, and you will know—if you follow the rhythm— the full, definitive exhaustion of thought. Let the tramps and Pozzo pummel you at the same time, and you will know what it is to be "finished!" Try keeping Hamm's chair *exactly* in the center of the stage, and you will know what a tortuous thing it is to wait on him. Try to hang yourself upon the tree—go ahead, try it—and you will see, decidedly, the degree to which the tree is useless. Eat Gogo's carrot and try to carry on a conversation and you will know quite materially that a carrot is a carrot.

On the physical level, the inexhaustibility of the plays is just plain exhausting. Even thinking is a physical task, not only for Lucky. Look at Didi's face agonized with the effort to use his intelligence. Our actors discovered the physical investment demanded of them in this apparently intellectual play, as they discovered a new conception of character-in-action. Indeed, Beckett has fulfilled on stage the idea of character advanced by Lawrence in his famous letter to Edward Garnett. Not character defined by "a certain moral scheme," but character as a "physiology of matter, . . . the same as the binding of the molecules of steel or their action in heat. . . ." Not what the character *feels*, for "that presumes an *ego* to feel with," but what the character "IS—inhumanly, physiologically, materially. . . ." Lawrence speaks of another ego with allotropic states, in which the individual goes through transformations "of the same radically unchanged element. (Like as diamond and coal are the same pure element of carbon. The ordinary novel would trace the history of diamond—but I say, 'Diamond, what! This is carbon!')"

Like Lawrence, Beckett is out to recover *wonder*, the mysterious harmony of man-in-nature, man-as-nature. But characteristically, like chipping a hairline in marble with a nib, he does this in the form which puts character—in all its flux and transformation—in *separate bodies* before you. By an act of histrionic juggling in which they perform no-action, the two tramps convince us they live one-life. Between them—urinating, eating carrots, putting on boots, scratching the head, playing charades—they compose an identity. While habit may be the great deadener, bare necessity gives energy. The rhythm is a continuum of crossed purposes and lapsed memory. How did they get that way? As Gogo says, unable to recall what happened the shortest time before: "I'm not a historian." For the actors, identity has to be rehearsed into being. As there is no biography, there is no other way.

Nevertheless, instead of demeaning men by reducing them to tramps in an inscrutable dependency, *Godot* restores the idea of heroism by making the universe their slave. They are, as Simone Weil says of Being (in a book with a title that describes the play, *Gravity and Grace*), "rooted in the absence of a place." What would it be without them? "To see a landscape as it is when I am not there," she muses. Unimaginable. "When I am in any place, I disturb the silence of heaven and earth by my breathing and the breathing of my heart."

Because the waiting, for all its avowed purpose, is purely gratuitous, it is bound to look comic—especially when, as with Pozzo, the heart seems to stop. If, like Chaplin, the tramps are victims too, there is a comparable sweetness in the terror. And unconscious power: Godot is concealed in their names.

The movement is circular, like a worn-out wheel of fortune at a deserted fairground, mysteriously turning. Having come out of history like shadows, the tramps are nothing but, and something more than, the concrete fact of the time they pass. And the question of Time in the theater is limned in their every gesture. Time-in-space. If the landscape needs one of them, the one needs the other. And, as we sit superior to their impotence, our whole past vibrates in their ready presence. Patience. The future stirs in the magic circle, wheels within wheels within wheels.

Do they also serve who only stand and wait? There is an exemplum in the stasis. To a country always in danger of floundering in its industry, *Godot* is a marvelous caution.

And with all its pretended anti-drama, we know it is brazenly theatrical—an occasion for Talent: the Nō, the pantomime, the music hall, the circus, the Greek messenger, and the medieval angel; the play is a history of dramatic art. There is even the Secret of the well-made play, Sardoodledom's ultimate question: Who is Godot? Will he come? But above all, there is Racine, the great dramatist of the closed system and the moral vacuum, salvaging exhausted *données*, illuminating what was at the beginning almost entirely known.

Someone cries, another weeps—by the sorcery of form Beckett defies the Second Law of Thermodynamics. Energy is pumped back into the dead system by having it come back from the other side of the stage, crippled and much the worse for wear, crying pitiably for help, and then behaving like an Ancient Hero, wisdom come from suffering:

> *Have you not done tormenting me with your accursed time! It's abominable! When! When! One day, is that not enough for you, one day he went dumb, one day I went blind, one day we'll go deaf, one day we were born, one day we shall die, the same day, the same second, is that not enough for you? (Calmer.) They give birth astride of a grave, the light gleams an instant, then it's night once more. (He jerks the rope.) On!*   [p. 57b]

In the great mystique of modern helplessness, Beckett's strange achievement is to provide us, exploring the rubble, with the most compelling theatrical image of the courage-to-be.

As character grows fabulous, so does nature—with the same

paucity of means. The tree grows leaves, the moon appears in an instant. In this effect and in the knockabout farce, there are similarities to Brecht, who admired the play and wanted to write an answer. The difference: Brecht's moon is hung on a chain; Beckett's "bleeds" out of the sky. If Alienation means to be made strange, coercing you to look again at the familiar, salvaging it from history, Beckett is the most conspicuous dramatist of Alienation. It is another way of describing his subject.

In discovering a style, the effort was to extend the natural into the unnatural, to create the reality of illusion *and* the illusion of reality, to make the theatrical real and the real theatrical, to test the very limits of style and stage. Thus, the actors, who might be going through the routine motions of anxiety, as natural as possible, would move, almost without transition, into the shoulder-to-shoulder, face-front attitude of burlesque comedians. Or Gogo, wandering about the stage in irritation, would suddenly strike the proscenium and cry: "I'm hungry!" The motive was personal, the extension theatrical, the biological urge becoming the aesthetic question. The proscenium had, in our production, no "real" place in the "environment" presumably established by the scenery, but it was an immovable fact in the topography of the stage. It was part of the theatrical environment as a painter's studio is an environment for his painting. Our task in performance was to make such gestures believable moments of action, to reassert the oldest criterion of dramatic truth, to make the improbable probable. Gogo's strike was a criticism, encapsulating years of protest, as if he'd be less hungry if the proscenium didn't exist. The character's problem, the actor's problem, the theater's problem, the philosophical problem were rolled into his fist.

Needless to say, the proscenium didn't fall.

When we played in New York, an actor who had studied truth objected to another extended gesture by saying, "People don't do it that way." What beguiled us—aside from his certainty about how people do what they do, the different conceptions of reality and style involved—was that he thought we didn't know it.

Godot, indeed, gives the definitive turn to the idea of Alienation. A subterranean drama, appearing to care for nothing but its interior life, it searches the audience like a Geiger counter. No modern drama is more sensitively aware of the presence of an audience, or its absence. There is this consciousness in its most delicate dying fall, when the actors are most intensely self-absorbed. Empathy is controlled with diabolic precision. The Chekhovian silences, the residue of aimless doing, are measured as carefully as in Webern. It is then, in silence, that the whole emotive tapestry of the theatrical event can be *heard*. The music is the most artful polyphony. Listen to the awakened boredom, the very heartbeat of the audience in this superb threnody on desire, mortality, and Time [p. 40b]. I am talking of *action-to-be-played*. Gogo and Didi are like dully dressed bower-birds in what the ornithologists call a "tight arena," absolutely attuned to each other, but waiting for someone else. Here they are actually engaged in a competition of sound and image, two *performers* trying to top each other, while character disappears in the metabolism. If nobody comes, together they are (the word was said with a beautifully syllabified sibilance) *sufficient*, constituting a rhythm. The rhythm is their bower. And as they sit side-by-side, staring out into the dark auditorium, listening to nothing, who can avoid hearing more of himself, and thus becoming a participant in the drama?

"The air is full of our cries," loudest in silence. To live is to be dubious, the acting is a revelation, we are all exposed: "At me too someone is looking, of me too someone is saying. . . ." The play-within-the-play was never so poignant, so particular, in its quiet dignity.

For our company, in the midst of the Silent Generation, Beckett's silence was a considerable shock. And the actor, associating through his own anxieties, had to submit to the rhythm. If *Waiting for Godot* was another testament to the decay of language, it was no mere pantomime of impoverished rhetoric, a mere autotelic gabble of words, words, words.

Beckett worked like an engraver or a diamond cutter. And in the best classical French tradition, he was purifying the language of the tribe, by referring words back to things, by making things of words. Despairing of communication, some of us were getting our kicks from silence. Thus catatonic jazz, thus dope, thus Zen. I don't mean to simplify these phenomena of the period, but Beckett knows well how deceitful, and lazy, they can be. His personal addiction is to the hardest task. "It is all very well to keep silence, but one has also to consider the kind of silence one keeps." As Roger Blin has pointed out, Beckett is not only prudish, but "In daily life we are confronted with a positive personality; a man who has fought indignities."

PREPARING FOR GODOT—
OR THE PURGATORY OF INDIVIDUALISM

DARKO SUVIN

Many students of Beckett have noted that his work is a radically foreshortened recapitulation of a certain cognitive and artistic tradition, almost a condensation of a segment of intellectual history. A few have gone so far as to identify that segment, usually at its source:

> . . . all Beckett's work paradoxically insists upon and rebels against the Cartesian definition of man as "a thing that thinks," (. . .) the Cartesian cleavage between the world in re and the world in intellectu . . .[1]

but sometimes as silt.

[1] R. Cohn, "Philosophical Fragments in the Works of Samuel Beckett," in *Samuel Beckett—A Collection of Critical Essays*, ed. M. Esslin (Englewood Cliffs, N.J.: Prentice-Hall, 1965), p. 170.

Comédie de Beckett, c'est Feydeau vu d'outre tombe.[2]

If Beckett's work is a "compendious abstract" of an epoch "chronicling the acquisition and dispersal of portable property, from Robinson Crusoe to The Spoils of Poynton,"[3] these terms should be accorded more attention by critics holding that (as the biologists put it) man's "inner environment" is genetically shaped by social more than by individual heredity. I propose to call that epoch by the central and stylistically decisive category of Individualism, i.e., vision, feeling, and cognition of World and Man from the standpoint of the Individual as the irreducible, atomic touchstone and measure. The world view of individualism arose at the time of Petrarch and Machiavelli in Italy, a century later in France and the Netherlands, and another century later in England.[4] There it found a striking literary exemplification in the archetypal figure of Robinson Crusoe on his desert island, justly felt as relevant to Beckett's propertyless Robinson pairs in their latter-day island-worlds.[5]

The centuries of Individualism between Descartes and Beckett are a time of the definitive victory of money economy over natural economy. This Instauratio Magna led to many and great triumphs of man over nature, but at a high, perhaps exorbitant price. The price of Individualist glories, of the new enterprising "Faustian"[6] spirit, may be summed up as the

---

[2] G. Sandier, quoted in P. Melèse, Samuel Beckett (Paris: 1966), p. 169.

[3] H. Kenner, Samuel Beckett: A Critical Study (New York: Grove Press, Inc., 1961), p. 63.

[4] I have devoted special studies to the nature, provenience, and relationship of Individualism to the Gothic and Renaissance period in the book Dva vida dramaturgije (Two Aspects of Dramaturgy), Zagreb, 1964, and in the essay "On Individualist World View in Drama," Les Problèmes des Genres Littéraires (Lodz) 1(16) 1966.

[5] Cf. besides Kenner, G. Anders, "Being Without Time," in Esslin, op. cit., p. 147.

[6] Cf. O. Spengler, Der Untergang des Abendlandes I (München: 1920); W. Sombart, Der moderne Kapitalismus I (München u. Leipzig: 1916); and G. Simmel, Philosophie des Geldes (München u. Leipzig: 1930).

dehumanizing processes of *desensualization* and *reification*. Desensualization of men's relations to material reality is a direct
result of the reduction of all commodities to the tyrannical
common denominator of money. All phenomena then appear as
reducible to quantitative measurement; all values, including
even God, can be treated as entries in an individual profit-and-
loss account. The *en gros* sale of indulgences—heavenly bliss or
at least purgatorial remittance for ready cash—which enraged
the sturdy sensitivity of Martin Luther, was only the logical
result of a general system where posthumous legacies were sup-
posted to atone for one's living usury. God is increasingly
treated as the owner of a huge and many-sided commercial firm,
"The World and Sons," differing in size but not in kind from
those of Bardi and Peruzzi, the Medicis or the Fuggers. All of
the middle class being God's children, He is accordingly each
one's potential senior partner.

ESTRAGON: *What exactly did we ask him for?* [...]
VLADIMIR: *Oh ... Nothing very definite.*
ESTRAGON: *A kind of prayer.*
VLADIMIR: *Precisely.*
ESTRAGON: *A vague supplication.*
VLADIMIR: *Exactly.*
ESTRAGON: *And what did he reply?*
VLADIMIR: *That he'd see.*
ESTRAGON: *That he couldn't promise anything.*
VLADIMIR: *That he'd have to think it over.*
ESTRAGON: *In the quiet of his home.*
VLADIMIR: *Consult his family.*
ESTRAGON: *His friends.*
VLADIMIR: *His agents.*
ESTRAGON: *His correspondents.*
VLADIMIR: *His books.*
ESTRAGON: *His bank account.*
VLADIMIR: *Before taking a decision.*
ESTRAGON: *It's the normal thing.*

VLADIMIR: *Is it not?*
ESTRAGON: *I think it is.*
VLADIMIR: *I think so too.*
    Silence.   [p. 13a]

In the balance sheet of individual life, the new "double-entry"
bookkeeping (*ragioneria*, systematized by Fra Pacioli in the
15th century) separates invested money from its natural-
economy function of acquiring objects necessary for life: in the
new system money acts autotelically, existing purely for quantitative self-propagation, which gave Christian writers a good
deal of trouble right up to the time of Ben Jonson.[7] All the
qualities of objects thus become irrelevant for commerce, which
sweeps away the limitations imposed by human nature and
personal needs (one can eat, wear out, etc., only so many
objects in a given time). The sensual data of cloth or cloves,
flour or color, surrender pride of place to the rational information about the amount of capital invested and profit earned,
which can be only larger or smaller: quantity becomes money's
only quality. Success in Individualist life manifests itself as the
size of the profit, with no direct sensual values involved. The
ideal capitalist thus should live privately in one world and
socially in another; he moves into a growing split between ambition and enjoyment, body and reason, feeling and thought, the
immanent and the transcendental. In the terminology of T. S.
Eliot—who was the first modern Anglo-American critic to
draw attention to these facts—his sensibility dissociates.[8]

The profit principle and the ideology of Rationalism meet on
the grounds of belief in omnipotent quantity—in the number.
The very term *ratio* (*ragione, raison*) slides from the classical
Ciceronian sense of "reason, relation, manner, calculation, ac-

---

[7] Cf. M. Weber, *The Protestant Ethic and the Spirit of Capitalism*
(London: 1958); R. H. Tawney, *Religion and the Rise of Capitalism*
(London: 1938); and L. C. Knights, *Drama and Society in the Age of
Jonson* (London: 1962).

[8] T. S. Eliot, "The Metaphysical Poets," *Selected Essays* (London:
1961).

count" into the sense of an entry (*conto*) in ledgers, and finally into that of a commercial establishment or concern. Rationalism means, quite literally, the ideology ("-ism") of business ("ratio"). It is not by chance that Individualism acquired a Rationalist philosophy, a Cartesian image of movement and a Newtonian cosmography. Double-entry bookkeeping introduced into daily economic life—the repository of social stereotypes—account entries which function as objects; once set into motion, such financial and numerical bodies move in calculable, mechanically determined grooves. Literary figures acquire analogous characteristics (compare Shakespeare and Ibsen), their actions are determined by calculation of profit or loss, whereas all other hypothetical motivations leave them inert. Finally, Beckett's figures find themselves in a permanent "Buridan's ass" type of tension between an ideal norm of rest (Nirvana, thermodynamic death) and motions caused bv flickers of the "hypothetical imperative," each motion meriting detailed description and deliberation as an aberration from the norm. Rationalism, analytic mathematics and mechanics are most intimately interwoven: in none of them is there a place for *qualities*, for fertile deviations from fixed positive laws. Fertility and vitality, divorced from the unique and the particular, become vested in institutionalized generalizations: just as the "legal person" of the enterprise grows distinct and separate from the sensual person of the *entrepreneur*, whom double-entry bookkeeping sees as a third party merely administering lent capital. A *fortiori*, other people too are interesting only rationally, as buyers or sellers of determined amounts of commodities (including their labor power) measurable in money and in time. Time, the measure of events, sluggish or non-existent in the feudal natural economy, becomes equivalent to finances and their ever swifter turnover. It was in the 14th century that amounts of time began to be measured exactly, and laments were heard over its lack and its rapid flow; all this moves with commerce, northward from Italy to England. From the financial emporium of Siena, St. Antoninus admits the subversive novelty of Time as a *"pretiosissima res et irre-*

cuperabilis,"[9] the first progenitor of the slogan "Time is money." Together with an unbounded mechanical space organized around individual nuclei of force, an arithmetic Time, neutral yet increasingly problematical, completes the Cartesian dimensions of analytical Individualist cosmography, where man sees man as a mere object of attraction or repulsion in time. Desensualized calculation encroaches upon fundamental human relationships such as producer to product, man to woman, parent to child. The brief interlude of a harmonious Renaissance whole of autonomous personalities—still visible in Boccaccio, Rabelais, or some comedies and romances of Shakespeare—draws to an abrupt close. Man can realize himself within such a flexible whole only as a specialized exploiter, "at the expense" of nature and other individuals. As Lucky has it, in the organizing backbone of his Speech on Man and Life:

. . . it is established beyond all doubt (. . .) that man in brief in spite of the strides of alimentation and defecation wastes and pines wastes and pines . . . [p. 29a]

In this context intimate contacts of one individual with another are increasingly fettered. Drama shows this very clearly: Shakespeare's socially unmotivated but full-blown figures can touch, clash, and harmonize; Diderot and Lessing already present only a pragmatic social morality of cooperation between individuals of a young and still oppositional class. Following this downward trajectory, Individualism arrives by way of the antisocial Romantic revolt (early Schiller, Hugo) to wholly egotistical moral Robinsons (realist drama). Finally, as the only possible connection between the desert islands of individual psyches, there remain psychotic conflicts—a connection by ground-to-ground missiles across seas of incommunicability (from Naturalists through Psychoanalysts to Psychopathologists, say Hauptmann—O'Neill—Williams). After all this Beckett has understandably preferred to leave his figures with-

---

[9] A. von Martin, *Soziologie der Renaissance* (Stuttgart: 1932), p. 119.

out any fetters, except those that are scenically functional. When Man is a Hobbesian wolf to Man, the realistic result is a ruthless defense of the Self and a denial of human solidarity. In throwing out the baby of a Man-to-Man relationship, figures such as Gogo and Didi may hope to get rid of the dirty bath of wolfishness.

Reification, the subordination of man to objects or things, is the second aspect of the price exacted by Individualism: within desensualized relationships *things* in their quantitativeness take pride of place. The arithmetic equivalents of things, *bodies,* and of their quantitative relations, *forces,* constitute the backbone of the clear and impoverished world-image of Rationalism. Here the ideal of plenty is no longer a stimulus for sensual enjoyment, as it was for Alberti, Leonardo, or Rabelais. No longer controlled by generic human values, quantitative abundance turns into an end in itself, running riot. Production divided from the producer is of bourgeois Individualist society—"the capital is independent and personal, while the active individual is dependent and impersonal."[10] Man, the producer and creator, is depersonalized on all fronts: economically (the capital), physically (the operation in the work process, soon mechanized), organizationally (the factory and its equivalents), legally (the company, increasingly anonymous in ownership and management), cognitively (specialization, later institutionalization), politically (the growing *apparati* of states and parties), and so forth. The dehumanized Leviathans of economics, society, State, correspond to a reified Man. In such a world the lay deity of things, commodities, possessions, dominates over a degraded personality. Beckett will try to escape this domination by rejecting things, while retaining and insisting on the degraded figures: results without causes make up the world of *Waiting for Godot.*

The Beckett world can thus be most usefully understood as a balance sheet which "takes stock . . . and reduces to essential

---

[10] K. Marx and F. Engels, *The Communist Manifesto,* Chapter II— my translation.

terms the three centuries, during which those ambitious processes of which Descartes is the symbol . . . accomplished the
dehumanization of man,"[11] in other terms the centuries of
Individualism. But what kind of reduction does this world
represent? Is it a laudatory or condemnatory balance of a judgment on the great Individualist tradition? The shying away
from any unique individual experience and its replacement by
reiterated, pseudo-allegorical events whose superimposition
creates an apparently timeless experience; indeed, the whole
savage degradation of world and man (a main theme of *Waiting for Godot*), which can be identified as a *reductio ad
absurdum* of Individualist relationships to their logical and
historical end-result—all such pointers leave little doubt of the
implied sardonic comment. Lucky's speech, or any number of
shorter examples, can be cited in proof.

The stance of a sardonic, condemnatory judgment on the
history of Individualism, its import, thought, and art, explains
the fact that, while bleakly abstracting its relationships, the
world of *Waiting for Godot* in some aspects harks back to pre-
Individualist forms and modes. For all its Newtonian inner
relations, this closed universe has a distinct affinity with the
Ptolemaic picture. It differs from that picture by being acutely
and dolorously, even morbidly conscious of at least a theoretical
possibility of transcendental vertical opening. Such a possibility
provides one of the poles of tension in the waiting for Godot.
This does not mean that such an opening implies—or that
Godot is to be equated with—a Christian, Buddhist, or any
other kind of God. I would feel that the closeness and distance
between Godot and God is exactly indicated by the names:
Godot is a kind of (small, impotent) god, who does not appear
to Gogo and Didi in that place where God used to be present
for Christians. Yet in his vanishing elusiveness Godot is at the
same time a pseudo-god, a surrogate of doubtful existentiality,
composed (even phonetically) out of the matter of the waiters;
he is functionally analogous to God, as gills are to lungs. How-

---

11 Kenner, *op. cit.*, p. 132.

ever, the constantly renewed comparison of a closed world with a possibility and foil of a different alternative is a fundamental device by means of which the encapsulated world of *Waiting for Godot* is felt as unnaturally small and oppressively claustrophobic.

For this island-universe is not only desolate but running down further. Objects, colors, energies are all in a state of degradation, visible as the cumulative fatigue of Gogo and Didi or the physical deterioration of Pozzo and Lucky, as a general "cascando" rhythm of the play as a whole and its particular situations. This universe tends asymptotically to an absolute lack of light, movement, and warmth—with which the *fin-de-siècle* physicists such as Boltzmann used to frighten a *fin-de-siècle* Europe.[12] Professor Kenner has wittily noted that the main characteristics of a Beckettian cosmos—a closed system and the degradation of its energy—are in fact the two laws of thermodynamics, as formulated in Newtonian physics. There remains unnoted, however, the third law of thermodynamics (Nernst's theorem: absolute zero can be approached only asymptotically, i.e., getting ever closer to it without ever reaching it), which is just as characteristic of Beckett's rhythm and vision in *Waiting for Godot*, and which should be accorded as important a place in any conclusion about it.

In such a world, where senselessness has radically blurred any clear aim, gestural and verbal action leads nowhere, moving in a peculiar repetitive shuttle:

ESTRAGON: (. . .) *Funny, the more you eat the worst it gets.*
VLADIMIR: *With me it's just the opposite.*
ESTRAGON: *In other words?*
VLADIMIR: *I get used to the muck as I go along.*
ESTRAGON: (after prolonged reflection). *Is that the opposite?*

[p. 14b]

---

12 For some examples, see C. Flammarion's novel *La Fin du Monde*, or H. G. Wells' *The Time Machine*.

Such a vicious circle repeated at length, turns exertion into stasis, human existence into an inconsequential nightmare, the passage of time into an effect of timelessness. It subjects the audience to disillusion at the end of each illusory period of achievement, of moving toward sense. In a way, *Waiting for Godot* could be pertinently discussed as a black parody of Renaissance "Comedies of Error," transposing their comic and joyous pairs into exemplary hopelessness—an inverted "As You (Dis)Like It."

The basic formal device of *Waiting for Godot* is a hesitating balance, without any clear leaning to either side. Godot is and is not God; consequently, the universe is and is not a closed one. Again, by the strange twilight-dialectics, this is and is not a living world. It is a zombie life-in-death or death-in-life territory, fauna and flora, an almost Lovecraftian fantasy, or a surreal limbo between being and non-being. With obvious reference to Dante's Purgatory (more particularly, as Beckett's interest in Belacqua proves, to the lowest "leap" of the Antepurgatory, where the negligent await the end of their punishment)—it is an inverted Purgatory, tending downward into hopelessness. In passing, I would venture the hypothesis that such Beckettian balance, and even many of its particular aspects, is an aesthetically specific expression of the present arrested balance in European and world history (and I do *not* mean the pragmatic balance between the great powers). At any rate, even a superficial glance at the whole structure of *Waiting for Godot*, its two acts, two pairs of figures, balancing neighboring and cross-act situations, the skeletal stichomythia, etc., points to the fundamental importance of this device. In some dialogues, even the central "indifferent" pointer of the balance can be clearly discerned, perhaps even graphically:

Vladimir: Now? . . .
(the posing of the question, setting the balance into motion)
    Joyous: There you are again . . .
        Indifferent: There we are again . . .
            Gloomy: There I am again.   [p. 38a]

(the balance, moving from left through the neutral position to right, in order to move in the next dialogue unit to the left again, hopefully; but the net effect is a resigned down-beat, it will be noticed).

Critical approaches to Beckett usually suppose him to be mirroring an existing state of reification and absurdity, finding his desert in an exact mirroring. Surprisingly rarely do they find his deserts in destructiveness, as: "He destroys in order to construct a city which never rises; but the space is cleared."[13] This implies a destroyer of the terrestrial City who clears the ground for the Heavenly City, which might be defined as the opposite of what he feels as horrible and ripe for destruction. This view of an anti-bourgeois St. Sam the Baptist is undoubtedly attractive to any criticism sympathetic to religious overtones, from Christian to some that passes for Marxian. What is more, up to a point it is quite plausible. Beckett did clear a lot of ground. For example, after *Waiting for Godot*, writing dramas like Eliot or Williams, Camus or latter Ionesco is no doubt still factually possible, but it can no longer be regarded as a significant artistic pursuit. In a wider context, his merciless devaluation of all Individualist values, his presentation of a depersonalized man and world certainly has some latent elements of social satire. Brecht was probably going to use this element in his first plans for an adaptation of *Waiting for Godot*, where the figures and their dialogues were to be socially anchored (Estragon becoming a worker, Vladimir an intellectual, Pozzo a large landowner, etc.).[14] Quite coherent performances of Beckett as a realistic warning can be given by emphasizing this aspect.

Yet compared, say, with Swift, the savage clowning of *Waiting for Godot* spurns any possibility of a radical transvaluation

---

[13] J. Jacobsen and W. R. Mueller, *The Testament of Samuel Beckett* (New York: Hill & Wang, 1964), p. 163.

[14] The main points of this adaptation have been quoted in W. Hecht, "Brecht 'und' Beckett," *Theater der Zeit* (East Berlin) 14/1966, but see also for reports on a later and different plan of adapting in K. Rülicke-Weiler, *Die Dramaturgie Brechts* (Berlin: 1966), pp. 154–56.

of Individualist values. Beckett demonstrates a valueless, de-humanized world; but in an almost dehumanized way, he lacks values in the name of which to resent such a world. His destruc-tiveness thus has the effect of abolishing all historical or tran-scendental horizons behind which a new City of the Sun may rise. Beckett's arrested Individualist and individual Purgatory is horribly godless because Individualist, and desperately frozen because Beckett is unable to believe in Individualism any longer. His own unhappy Rationalist consciousness is con-tinually faced with a paradox that is insoluble from within the Individualist frame:

> I speak of an art turning from the plane of the feasible in disgust, weary of its puny exploits, weary of pretending to be able, of being able, of doing a little better the same old thing, of going a little further along a dreary road.

The Beckett of *Three Dialogues* and *Waiting for Godot*, pre-fers to that art an "expression" in which the consciousness that "there is nothing to express" (within the Individualist tradition, I would add) joins hands with an equally strong consciousness of "the obligation to express."[15] Hence the balancing act: the Self, final atom of the Individualist world, has been broken up, leaving a void; yet the Individualist tradition of Self-questioning goes on undaunted, dryly enclosing the void.

---

[15] Samuel Beckett, Georges Duthuit and Jacques Putnam, *Bram van Velde: Three Dialogues* (New York: Grove Press, Inc., 1960).

WAITING FOR GODOT

G. S. FRASER

The fundamental imagery of *Waiting for Godot* is Christian; for, at the depth of experience into which Mr. Beckett is probing, there is no other source of imagery for him to draw on. His heroes are two tramps, who have come from nowhere in particular and have nowhere in particular to go. Their life is a state of apparently fruitless expectation. They receive messages, through a little boy, from the local landowner, Godot, who is always going to come in person tomorrow, but never does come. Their attitude toward Godot is one partly of hope, partly of fear. The orthodoxy of this symbolism, from a Christian point of view, is obvious. The tramps with their rags and their misery represent the fallen state of man. The squalor of their surroundings, their lack of a "stake in the world," represent the idea that here in this world we can build no abiding city. The ambiguity of their attitude toward Godot, their mingled hope and fear, the doubtful tone of the boy's messages, represents the state of tension and uncertainty in which the average Christian must live in this world, avoiding presumption, and also avoiding despair. Yet the two tramps, Didi and Gogo, as they call each other, represent something far higher than the other two characters in the play, the masterful and ridiculous Pozzo and his terrifying slave, Lucky. Didi and Gogo stand for the contemplative life. Pozzo and Lucky stand for the life of practical action taken, mistakenly, as an end in itself. Pozzo's blindness and Lucky's dumbness in the second act rub this point in. The so-called practical man, the man of action, has to be set on his feet and put on his way by the contemplative man. He depends—as becomes clear, in the first act, from Pozzo's genuine though absurd gratitude for the chance of a little conversation—on the contemplative man for such moments of insight, of spiritual communication,

From *The Times Literary Supplement*, February 10, 1956, where the material appeared anonymously. Reprinted by permission.

as occur in his life. The mere and pure man of action, the comic caricature of the Nietzschean superman, Pozzo, is like an actor who does not properly exist without his audience; but his audience are also, in a sense, his judges. Pozzo and Lucky, in fact, have the same sort of function in *Waiting for Godot* as Vanity Fair in *The Pilgrim's Progress*. But they are, as it were, a perambulating Vanity Fair; Didi and Gogo are static pilgrims. It is worth noting, also, that Didi and Gogo are bound to each other by something that it is not absurd to call charity. They treat each other with consideration and compunction (their odd relationship, always tugging away from each other, but always drawn together again, is among other things an emblem of marriage). Pozzo and Lucky are drawn together by hate and fear. Their lot is increasing misery; but if Didi and Gogo are not obviously any better off at the end of the play than they were at the beginning, neither are they obviously any worse off. Their state remains one of expectation.

Waiting for Godot . . . is a modern morality play, on permanent Christian themes. But, even if the Christian basis of the structure were not obvious, Mr. Beckett is constantly underlining it for us in the incidental symbolism and the dialogue. The first piece of serious dialogue in the play, the first statement, as it were, of a theme, is about the "two thieves, crucified at the same time as our Saviour." . . . The discussion goes on to canvass the melancholy possibility that perhaps both thieves were damned. And the effect of the dialogue on the stage is, momentarily, to make us identify the glib Didi and the resentful and inarticulate Gogo with the two thieves, and to see, in each of them, an overmastering concern with the other's salvation. There is also toward the end of the first act a discussion about whether their human affection for each other may have stood in the way of that salvation:

> ESTRAGON: *Wait!* (He moves away from VLADIMIR.) *I sometimes wonder if we wouldn't have been better off alone, each one for himself.* (He crosses the stage and sits down on the mound.) *We weren't made for the same road.*

VLADIMIR (without anger): *It's not certain.*
ESTRAGON: *No, nothing is certain.*   [*pp. 35a-35b*]

The tree on the stage, though it is a willow, obviously stands
both for the Tree of the Knowledge of Good and Evil (and, when
it puts on green leaves, for the Tree of Life) and for the Cross.
When Didi and Gogo are frightened in the second act, the best
thing they can think of doing is to shelter under its base. But
it gives no concealment, and it is perhaps partly from God's
wrath that they are hiding; for it is also the Tree of Judas, on
which they are recurrently tempted to hang themselves.

Here, in fact, we have the subtle novelty, the differentiating
quality, of *Waiting for Godot,* when we compare it with *Every-
man* or with *The Pilgrim's Progress.* Didi and Gogo do not
complete their pilgrimage nor are we meant to be clear that
they will complete it successfully. The angel who appears to
them at the end of the first act is an ambiguous angel: the angel
who keeps the goats, not the angel who keeps the sheep. And
Godot—one remembers that God chastises those whom he
loves, while hardening the hearts of impenitent sinners by al-
lowing them a term of apparent impunity—does not beat him
but beats his brother who keeps the sheep. . . . Are Didi and
Gogo in the end to be among the goats? The boy who appears
as a messenger at the end of the second act looks like the same
boy, but is not, or at least does not recognize them. He may be,
this time, the angel who keeps the sheep. That Godot himself
stands for an anthropomorphic image of God is obvious. That
is why Vladimir—if he had a blond or a black beard he might
be more reassuringly man or devil—is so alarmed in the second
act when he hears that Godot, Ancient of Days, has a white
beard. . . .

The peculiar bitter ambiguity of the use of the Christian
material is most obvious, perhaps, in the dialogue about Gogo's
boots toward the end of the first act:

VLADIMIR: *But you can't go barefoot!*
ESTRAGON: *Christ did.*

VLADIMIR: *Christt! What has Christ got to do with it? You're not going to compare yourself to Christ!*

ESTRAGON: *All my life I've compared myself to him.*

VLADIMIR: *But where he lived it was warm, it was dry!*

ESTRAGON: *Yes. And they crucified quick.*   [p. 34b]

One main function of Pozzo and Lucky in the play is to present, and to be the occasion of the dismissal of, what might be called "alternative philosophies." Pozzo, in the first act, is a man of power, who eloquently—too consciously eloquently, as he knows—expounds Nietzschean pessimism:

> *But*—(hand raised in admonition)—*but behind this veil of gentleness and peace night is charging* (vibrantly) *and will burst upon us* (snaps his fingers) *pop! like that!* (his inspiration leaves him) *just when we least expect it.* (Silence. Gloomily.) *That's how it is on this bitch of an earth.*
>
> [p. 25b]

Like an actor, he asks for applause. . . . In the second act, in his far more genuinely desperate state, his pessimistic eloquence is less obviously "theatrical":

> (Calmer.) *They give birth astride of a grave, the light gleams an instant, then it's night once more.* (He jerks the rope.) *On!*   [p. 57b]

There is an echo in the rhythm and idiom of the first sentence, there, of Synge. And since it is the only overtly "poetical" sentence which Mr. Beckett allows himself in this play, and since he is the most calculatingly skillful of writers, one may take it that the echo is meant as a criticism of Pozzo—a criticism of romantic stylized pessimism. If the Nietzschean attitude is dismissed in Pozzo, it is harder to suggest just what is dismissed in Lucky. He is the proletarian, who used to be the peasant. He used to dance "the farandole, the fling, the brawl, the jig, the fandango, and even the hornpipe." Now all he can dance are a few awkward steps of a dance called "the Net." But in

Lucky's long speech—the most terrifyingly effective single sustained episode in the play—he stands for a contemporary reality, composite, perhaps, but when presented to us immediately recognizable. He stands for half-baked knowledge, undigested knowledge, the plain man's naive belief in a Goddess called Science, his muddled appeals to unreal authorities [for] almost two complete pages! Lucky's speech is the great bravura piece of writing in the play. Mr. Beckett has never been more brilliantly unreadable; not only Didi, Gogo, and Pozzo but the audience want to scream. What is dismissed in Lucky's speech is perhaps Liberalism, Progress, Popular Education, what Thomas Love Peacock used to call, sardonically, "the March of Mind." The Nietzschean and the Liberal hypotheses being put out of court, the Christian hypothesis is left holding the stage. It is at least a more comprehensive and profound hypothesis, whatever Mr. Beckett may personally think of it; and the total effect of his play, therefore—since most of us, in the ordinary affairs of the world, have more of Pozzo or Lucky in us, than of Didi or Gogo—is not to lower but unexpectedly to raise our idea of our human dignity, even though expectations are never satisfied, and even though the most fundamentally important questions can expect, perhaps, at the most an implicit answer.

WAITING FOR GODOT: MYTH, WORDS, WAIT

ROBERT CHAMPIGNY

The three words of the original French title of Beckett's play *En attendant Godot* can be used to introduce the three per-

From *PMLA* (1960), reprinted by permission of the author and of the Modern Language Association. Translated from the French by Ruby Cohn, with revisions by the author.

spectives of this interpretation. The word *Godot* prompts an examination of the role of mythology in the play. While (*en* in French) waiting for Godot, the characters talk, and we shall examine their use of language. It will then remain for us to bring in the *waiting*, the existential background which the theatrical mask of myth and words does not manage to hide.

The characters of *Waiting for Godot* are presented as children of our century, or, more broadly, of an age which has often been characterized by the death of the sacred. However, myth has not disappeared, but has multiplied. And it is this multiplication which undermines its sacred character. Thus, to the old theological myth, evolutionary myths have been added. In such myths, which are biological or sociological in flavor, "Man" or "Mankind" is the name of the mythical protagonist. In Beckett's play, the Pozzo-Lucky couple is related to the modern type of myth, while the Vladimir-Estragon couple is related to the older kind.

Myth

Pozzo is the master and leader of the Pozzo-Lucky couple. He belongs to the ruling class whose function is to maintain a sociological myth. Since sociological myth rests upon history and not eternity, Pozzo doesn't want time to stop. Replying to the names, Abel and Cain, "He's all humanity." He takes the destiny of mankind upon himself. Pozzo is leading Lucky toward a mythical future (in the French version to the village named "Holy Savior"); to sell him, to be sure, since it is fitting that Pozzo, in his role of dictator, show scorn for the slave.

The common man is not idealized in the character of Lucky. Pozzo says that Lucky is wicked with strangers, and the latter proves it by biting Estragon, who was once a poet. Lucky is nothing like Shelley's Demogorgon; and Pozzo is a Prometheus who has become a new Jupiter. Hegel's dialectic of master and slave has lost its dynamism. Lucky merely desires to play the role of Lucky, and to do this he needs Pozzo in the role of Pozzo. Both actors attempt to play their parts convincingly: "Such an old and faithful servant . . . such a good master."

These are theatrical roles. Pozzo lives only for another actor (Lucky) or spectators (Vladimir, Estragon): his role is one of power, and he finds it difficult to reconcile his existential weakness and his theatrical strength. Even when we first see him, he is weary of a role which no longer fits him. Relativist opinions escape from him: "Let us not then speak ill of our generation, it is not any unhappier than its predecessors. (*Pause.*) Let us not speak well of it either. (*Pause.*) Let us not speak of it at all." [p. 22a] The common man, too, is weary of his role. Lucky can no longer dance "the Net. He thinks he's entangled in a net." As for thinking, Lucky can no longer manage revolutionary thought, but a theologico-scientific mishmash which he spits up without understanding. In Act II, Pozzo is blind, Lucky dumb. There has been complete disintegration of the mythological burden of the couple, that torch which is transmitted from generation to generation by edifying discourse: "What is there in the bag? Sand." The Act I implications of evolution and progress are replaced in Act II by circularity and by movement for its own sake: "[. . .] one day we were born, one day we shall die, the same day, the same second, is that not enough for you? . . . They give birth astride of a grave, the light gleams an instant, then it's night once more. . . . On!" [p. 57b]

Estragon and Vladimir try to form a spiritual brotherhood outside of society, turning toward theological myth. They meet each evening to live their sacred life, to celebrate a rite which consists mostly of *talking* about waiting for Godot. Society is an anonymous mass: "And they didn't beat you? Beat me? Certainly they beat me. The same lot as usual? The same? I don't know." As they seek to lose their ties to society, so the couple seeks to lose the social concept of time. They wish to separate their religious life from their profane life and to commune in the wait for a god.

These "intellectuals" no longer trust thought; is it anything other than the broken record illustrated by Lucky? At one point, there is a vague desire to commit oneself: "Let us not waste our time in idle discourse! . . . It is not every day that we are needed." [p. 51a] But the impulse fades quickly: "It is true that when with folded arms we weigh the pros and cons we are no less a credit to our species . . . Yes, in this immense confusion one thing alone is clear. We are waiting for Godot to come—" [pp. 51a-51b] They turn toward the religious theme of salvation, of the god who is going to come.

They are waiting for Godot. What bothers them is not a doubt about his existence, or even that he will always come "tomorrow" (that is to say, never); that is in the rules of the game. But they are waiting for a new god, and Godot is unfortunately reminiscent of the old kind of god, e.g., Jupiter, or Caesar (Pozzo). This echoes the resemblance between modern myths and theological myths: many people speak of a new religion, but nobody seems capable of inventing a religion that differs from the old ones. Unlike Blake, Estragon and Vladimir are incapable of inventing a poetic myth; even though they are somewhat contemptuous of one another (each seeing in the other a mirror of his own impotence), they need one another to bolster their tottering myth of Godot.

Early in the play, Godot is evoked as a businessman. Then Estragon mistakes Pozzo for Godot. Godot treats his messengers as highhandedly as does a human master. The messenger doesn't recognize Vladimir from one evening to the next, calling him, "Mister Albert." Is this the "divine" name of Vladimir? Or is the boy's message intended for someone else, who would be the "good" thief? Is that what Vladimir has in mind? I would prefer the following interpretation: Estragon and Vladimir try to die to this world, but eternity offers them no compensation. The climax to their disappointment occurs with the boy's announcement that Godot's beard is white.

Words

Dramatic characters can be realized only by gestures, mostly verbal. An awareness of this condition is felt in Waiting for Godot: "Return the ball"; also the awareness of lack of authenticity: "We always find something, eh Didi, to give us the impression we exist?" [p. 44b] Theatrical self-consciousness can be found in the works of other modern dramatists: in Pirandello, Anouilh, Sartre, and most conspicuously in Genet. From the standpoint of the playwright, this tendency may be summarized as follows: the theater represents life in so far as life is theatrical, but what is theatrical in life is inauthentic; therefore, let us write anti-theatrical plays.

The contemporary situation of common language contributes to this theatrical self-consciousness. Common language shows signs of decomposition. Various technical terms and patterns invade speech, and yet traditional terms and patterns do not vanish. The multiplicity of "truths," the shower of slogans, helps loosen the mask of language. For Vladimir and Estragon, and even for Pozzo, language is no longer an idol, but neither is it a tool or a toy. Rather it consists of fragments of broken idols, tools, and toys. The characters toss out a theme, a kind of verbal montage, and then they abandon it. Beckett's technique might be called a broken symbolism, for he suggests a symbolic diagram, then destroys it. We are reminded of Joyce's necropolis of symbols, and even more of Wittgenstein's analysis of language.

Our rights, "we got rid of them," says Vladimir, who can no longer let himself be caught in a socio-verbal role. "We're not tied?" asks Estragon, who has been a poet (surrealist?). Language has come loose: "What is terrible is to *have* thought. But did that ever happen to us?" I would interpret this to mean that thinking with words causes a loss of innocence, the process ending with the question: what does the word "thought" mean? Estragon and Vladimir give a semblance of life back to "dead voices." "To have lived is not enough for them. They have to talk about it." I talk, therefore I am (a *persona*). Estragon and Vladimir are in search of characters: "We could play at Pozzo and Lucky." Verbal masks no longer express emotions: "Say, I am happy. I am happy . . . What do we do now, now that we're happy?"

These remarks do not hold true for Lucky, for whom language is still an idol. He alone can "think," that is to say, he speaks seriously, seeming to believe in it. However, he can only speak the language he has learned—a contemporary pot-pourri larded with theological and scientific phrases. An indiscriminate learning-machine, Lucky adopts an attitude of belief, but the incoherence of the lesson robs believing itself of content.

"That's been going on now for half a century." The first half of the twentieth century has been described as a crisis in language. The characters are old. They are still attached to a mythological way of thinking, but they can neither commit themselves to old myths nor invent a new one. They cannot invent a language without a myth, but they cannot do without language. They are fastened to the stage of a theater, which they recognize as such: "Let's go. We can't. Why not? We're waiting for Godot." Thus, we return to the title.

Wait

Both language and mythology reveal the negative meaning of the play. If we stopped our analysis there, we would see the play as pessimistic or nihilistic. But the work, which is at least as comic as it is tragic, invites us to throw off this spirit of seriousness. The theater represents life to the extent that life is theatrical. The play's nihilism attacks a conception which reduces life to the theater, existence to myth. In other words, the play attacks a conception which would cramp life into a metaphysical box. Thus, the play is an implicit critique of an essentialist conception. Like Beckett's novel *The Unnamable*, the play might be interpreted as an anti-Cartesian meditation. Here too, one starts with the *tabula rasa,* but Beckett refuses both the mask of the self and the mask of a god.

Beckett is careful to show the limits of theater. Vladimir and Estragon speak of suicide, but they do not hang themselves from the tree. Language may be separated from life, but life is riveted to the body. What can the play tell us beyond theatrical representation?

There are two possible alternatives to the wait for Godot. One is suicide, the supreme act: "We'll hang ourselves tomorrow. Unless Godot comes." That act, in contrast to speaking about it, would force us out of the theater. The second possible alternative is to wait for night to fall: "We are waiting for Godot to come . . . Or for night to fall." That night might be, will be, death; or one might interpret it as a mystic night. Words and things disappear before the simple and permanent *there-is*.

Estragon and Vladimir seem to desire this: "This is becoming really insignificant. Not enough." They destroy language with words. But they are confined to this verbal negation. They remain on stage, inseparable actors. Action and contemplation are suggested, but the characters cannot escape the realm of what is only gesture.

On stage, there is the tree: "Everything's dead but the tree." The tree of life is on stage, and yet it is not in the play. Similarly, though "waiting for Godot" is theatrical, the wait itself is not, beneath all the words. The dissolution of myths and verbal masks reveals existential reality, the wait. The play gradually accomplishes this existential reduction, especially as suggested by the following words: "waiting for night, waiting for Godot, waiting for . . . waiting." One might say that "Godot" and "night" cancel each other out, and the wait remains.

The play's meaning is thus comparable to Sartre's *Nausea* or Camus' *The Stranger*. In all of these works, existential reality is revealed with the help of words, in spite of words, and beyond words. In Beckett's play, it is waiting that shows existential reality; not waiting for this or that, but waiting; not Time as a form of cognitive thought, but the wait as lived, out of time; not hope or desire or fear, but undifferentiated waiting. This wait is the basic way to live what-has-to-be-lived, the gerundive aspect of existence. Thus, there can be neither optimism nor pessimism, since life must be lived, and that is all. If life makes no sense, it is because life *is* sense.

Under the pressures of technology, our age may destroy not only a given myth or ideology, but the very spirit of mythology and ideology. And that is where the significance of *Waiting for Godot* is most valid, since it does not redecorate a given mythology, nor sketch a new one; it does not even ask for a new one. Beyond its theatrical aspect, the play tries to suggest what is existentially authentic for the animal with language.

ART AND THE EXISTENTIAL IN
WAITING FOR GODOT

LAWRENCE E. HARVEY

1. The Given World: Compartments, Patterns, and Surfaces

The starting point in *Godot*, the given world that is to be transformed, is less easily describable than in more naturalistic works, since, as we see it, it is already well along in the process of dissolution. Its existence, however, is at least implicit in almost every line of the play, and from its scattered remnants it is not too difficult to reconstruct the original, our own surprisingly familiar modern world. This is a world in which clock time plays an extremely important part, and the clock never stops. We busily organize our ac.. ''es and our rendezvous chronometrically and, like Pozzo, check our watches frequently to make sure we are in the proper temporal compartment. Localization in space is almost as important. We are Italians, Englishmen, Russians, Frenchmen, etc. . . .

What kinds of people inhabit these temporal and spatial compartments? Specialists: successful businessmen, aristocrats, intellectuals, researchers, metaphysicians, anthropologists, medical men, nutrition experts, sanitary engineers, a few poets, and tremendous numbers of sports enthusiasts. A great deal of time is spent in conversation and speech making. We are very polite and usually apologize effusively after our discussions, as occa-

---

From *PMLA* (1960), abridged with the author's approval. Reprinted by permission of the Modern Language Association.

sionally happens, have become overheated. We believe in progress, adhere to the teachings of the Christian religion, and are generally hopeful and optimistic. We work, enjoy sex, are often gourmets, and are quite interested in fashions in clothes. We believe in liberty, equality, and fraternity, are respectful of others, even our inferiors, have a veritable cult of sympathy, are charitable and selfless. We are happy, busy people with no time for loneliness, and we do not really believe in suffering, old age, or death.

2. The Erosive Power of Art

The negative action of the artistic process operates on this world, or one that very closely resembles it, and tends to reduce it to the status of an insubstantial surface, an illusory façade. The frequent memory failures of the various characters break the continuity of linear time, to which modern Western society is so accustomed. The impression is created that there is no causal relationship, nor even marked differences, between past and present, which therefore tend to merge into each other. . . .

Another means of destroying our sense of linear or progressive time is by the introduction of the circle. Metaphorically, any return to a given starting point may evoke the idea of circularity, and to this end the innumerable repetitions and returns to early phrases, motifs, and situations serve very effectively. More explicit is the stage direction "looking around." The broken record is imitated several times in Lucky's speech, . . . and on one occasion, thinking themselves surrounded, Vladimir and Estragon seek to escape in four different directions only to realize that there is no exit. At the beginning of Act II Vladimir is singing a round song. . . .

Lucky, when he begins to "think," not only deflates the intellectual but at the same time satirizes into non-existence our many specialized professional and avocational categories. The dignified anthropology becomes the comical anthropometrics and is further ridiculed by the stuttering repetition of the central syllable, Anthropopopometry. In a more general way, the

modern institution of the Academy that awards prizes for ex-
cellence in the various fields becomes the Acacacacademy,
which by implication dispenses *caca* (excrement in child language) for unfinished research. . . .

According to Beckett the proliferation of words in the
modern world does not necessarily imply communication between people. Often the so-called dialogue between Vladimir
and Estragon degenerates into two monologues. The French
mania for the *conférence*, which we share, is beautifully caricatured in the public addresses of the atomizer-carrying Pozzo.
Our surface etiquette and professed respect for others is met in
Godot by the verbal and physical brutality of Pozzo toward
Lucky. Estragon comments on the depth of our religious beliefs
when he says, as Vladimir brings up the subject of salvation
and damnation, "I'm going." [p. 9a] The myth of progress falls
in Lucky's speech, in which we learn that man, in spite of vita-
mins, sanitation, penicillin, and physical education, is in the
process of shrinking. It is quite significant that this shrinking
dates from the time of Voltaire who stands, here, for the century that believed too naively in the dream of human progress
and probably, as well, for a time of surfaces, surfaces that
Beckett is out to destroy. He reduces our gourmet delicacies to
carrots, black radishes, and that staple of the starvation time
under the German occupation, the lowly turnip. Our sex life
leads to venereal disease; our laughter is silenced in pain; our
fashionable clothes turn into rags, our lithe youth into stum-
bling old age, and our busy lives into a solitary waiting for
death. We are not free but bound to each other and Godot; we
are not equal but exist in a series of compartments in the social
hierarchy; even our feelings of charity and fraternity are hesi-
tant and fearful and inspired chiefly by our own selfish needs.
As for our cult of sympathy, a quality that does little to remedy
human suffering, Lucky's angry kick is the best commentary.

Of all the patterns of this given world that dissolve in the
acid-bath of Beckett's art none is more pervasive and controlling
than language. Here I should like to repeat the well-known
"anecdote of a Tyrolian German discussing with a Tyrolian

Italian the merits of their respective languages. . . . The German brings the discussion to a close with the remark: 'You call *Pferd* a *cavallo* but it *is* a *Pferd*'!"[1] Anyone who teaches a foreign language is well aware of this prevalent confusion between language and reality. Perhaps the speech of Lucky is the most obvious instance of Beckett's attack on conventional language. Here sentence and paragraph structure give way to thematic organization. Several topics develop in a more or less causal fashion but their progress is impeded by the periodic recurrence of a number of leitmotivs, by overlapping, and by recall of earlier stages in the development. It is quite possible to distinguish a degenerate form of our logical discourse in this speech—and this reflects the degeneration of Lucky's intelligence—but this dynamic mode is subordinated to a static pattern of thematic repetition, which mirrors Beckett's existential preoccupations.

A general device for undermining the stability of the world as we know it is formal or semantic ambivalence. Estragon points out that the English say *cawm* instead of *calm* and suggests that they must be cawm people, implying naively that there may be a difference between cawm and calm people. At another point he uses French: "Oh tray bong, tray tray tray bong." [p. 25b] This is neither an interest in local color nor merely an easy way to get a laugh from the audience. It is rather a means of calling into question the reality of language. One symbol may be mistaken for the thing itself. Two, in a sense, cancel each other out and enable reality to disengage itself from language. We may be sure that the person is something more than the name when we hear Lucky's master called Pozzo, Bozzo, and Gozzo. Is the rendezvous with Godot, Godet, or Godin? Does Pozzo smoke a pipe, a briar, a dudeen, or a Kapp and Peterson? What is it that he carries about with him, a vaporizer, spray, or pulverizer? . . . Does the divinity reign from the heights of his apathia, athambia, or aphasia? Such uncertainty permeates the

---

[1] Reported by Leo Spitzer in "Language of Poetry" in *Language: An Enquiry into its Meaning and Function*, ed. Ruth N. Anshen (New York: Harper & Brothers, 1957), p. 202.

whole play. We are asked to doubt whether one of the two crucified thieves was saved or whether both were damned. We wonder whether Godot will come or not, whether his messenger is the same or a different boy, whether we are bound to him, whether he is kind or cruel, what will happen when and if he does come. Such a state of general uncertainty would be impossible without the prior destruction of the many conventional, and often arbitrary, patterns within the comfortable limits of which we live, and which may keep us from coming to grips with the hard reality that is the human condition. And this brings us to the next stage in the artistic process.

3. Beneath the Surfaces

". . . habit," says Vladimir, "is a great deadener." [p. 58b] What then do we hear when the great mute is destroyed? At first, there is only silence, emptiness, immobility, boredom, and waiting. Soon, however, sounds begin to become audible. Listening, bent over his own watch pocket, for his lost timepiece, Pozzo hears nothing. He is joined by Vladimir and Estragon. "I hear something," says Estragon. It is not the tick-tock of the watch, however, but the sound of the human heart. Chronometric time has been replaced by existential time.[2] This movement from surface to underlying reality brings us, when space is the category, to the same obsessive vision: "You and your landscapes! Tell me about the worms!" [p. 39b] In one of the most striking and significant scenes in the play, a central image is acted out by Pozzo, the image of the course of day, figuring, as it so often has, the course of man's life. Beckett signals the importance of the passage by stylizing gestures and language.

---

[2] In order to avoid any possible misunderstanding, let me repeat here a convenient distinction, set forth by Robert Champigny in "Existentialism and the Modern French Novel" (*Thought*, XXXI, CXXII, Autumn, 1956), between existentialist literature, in which "fundamental themes are deliberately linked to an existential philosophy" (p. 367), and existential literature which has to do with the human condition and man's fate but which lacks such a direct link. This study is concerned only with the existential nature of Beckett's play.

He further sets off the lyric tone by an occasional word to be said in an especially prosaic way. [pp. 25a and b] . . .

Beckett has, again and again, bent apparently linear chronometric time into the static form of the circle. . . . Against the monotony of the circle is set the fearful descending line that ends in the grave. Perhaps nowhere in the play is this combination of static and dynamic suggested more vividly than in Vladimir's round song. The circular pattern is interrupted, momentarily at first, when the singer comes to the lines, "Then all the dogs came running/And dug the dog a tomb . . ." [p. 37a] He repeats the two lines and goes on to complete the circle. On the second time around, however, he is stopped again. This time he repeats the two lines, then the second line again, *softly*, and the song ends in silence and immobility (*"He remains a moment silent and motionless . . ."*) that seems almost an imitation of the meaning evoked by the words. The surface circularity has been broken again in order to expose the terrible linear direction of man's destiny.

The manifestations of this line are many in the play. In Lucky's speech man has grown thinner, shorter, and generally smaller. Lucky himself has degenerated in his ability to dance and to think. During the course of the play all the characters find it more and more difficult to stand up. One by one Pozzo loses articles of the paraphernalia he carries with him on his journey. His whip loses its crack and he much of his confident superiority. From master and slave driver he becomes a helpless blindman led by a deaf guide. Vladimir and Estragon might at one time have been among the first to jump off the Eiffel tower. Now they would not even be allowed to go up. The sucked chicken bones are likened later to fish bones; the more you eat of the carrot, the worse it gets. The carrot, succulent at least toward the tender end, is replaced later by a radish, not a radish of the former rose-colored variety but a black one. The second pipe is always inferior to the first. In acting out his lyric scene Pozzo says, "I weakened a little towards the end. . . ." [p. 25b] Even in details like tones of voice indicated in the stage directions, this movement is evident. At one point, Vladimir repeats, with variations, the same idea, first joyously, "There you are again," then indifferently, "There we are again," and at last gloomily, "There I am again." [p. 38a]

A number of other aspects of the existential become apparent when the surfaces are shattered: fear, suffering, ignorance, man's incompatibility with his environment, unhappiness, fatigue, loneliness, need, and dreams which may imitate reality in the nightmare of falling (but which may, on the other hand, be an escape into the illusion of happiness that blinds us to the suffering of our fellows). The basic biological needs, the rudimentary physical facts of existence, also take on an increased importance. . . . Linked to all these things, and therefore in a way the most terrifying of all, into the void left by the destruction of the patterns comes thought, drawn as by a magnet toward the idea of man's fate. The dead thoughts of the past are metamorphosed into cadavers and bones in a great cemetery, which, as though magnetized itself, pulls the eye toward it. "You don't have to look," says Estragon. "You can't help looking," replies Vladimir. [p. 41b] Into the void too come some feelings, however mixed, of charity and fraternity, and the small hope that, aided sometimes by fear, keeps men either waiting for Godot or struggling on toward Saint-Sauveur. It is hardly Dante's "present certainty of future happiness," but it is a kind of hope nonetheless.

In his article on the language of poetry, Leo Spitzer wrote of the representative potential of the number two. In such expressions as "it rains and rains," for example, ". . . language has chosen only two links in the chain, which are called upon to represent the infinite expansion (rains and rains and rains and rains, etc.)."[3] This idea, it seems to me, explains beautifully the overall structure of *Waiting for Godot* with its two acts that portray two days in a long series. One act would be too few, three too many. The single repetition suffices to evoke the monotonous recurrence inherent in the human condition. We have seen the destructive powers of one juxtaposed to one. Such

---

[3] Spitzer, *op. cit.*, p. 205.

juxtapositions have their positive side as well, since two speeches are enough to make possible an expansion to the universal and existential. Cain plus Abel = Pozzo or, as Estragon says, "all humanity," man the sufferer and the cause of suffering. In an extension of the same process, the many national types doing research reduce to man seeking knowledge about his fate, and the various national dances to three, "The Scapegoat's Agony," "The Hard Stool," and "The Net." [p. 27a] It is unnecessary for the author to indicate further that these in turn reduce to a single dance, the "danse macabre." The extensive use of repetition, recall, and parallelism, in the final analysis, calls into play this same principle. Once the basic method is well established, Beckett can even go so far as to omit parts, even the essential parts, of a recurrent phrase, thereby forcing the audience into an active role in the expansion to the existential. "All that's a lot of bloody—" [p. 43b] remains unfinished, and the reader must fish back into his own memory for the important missing word, "lies." [p. 33a]. . . .

Beckett employs often a kind of stubborn repetition, and usually this is a signal heralding a particularly significant theme. "Why doesn't he put down his bags?" [pp. 17a, 20a, 21a] and "You want to get rid of him?" [pp. 21a and b, seven times] certainly have extra-literal implications. Suffering is involved, perhaps the question of suicide, and no doubt the Godot-man relationship, analogous to the master-slave tie that links Pozzo and Lucky. What might be called the technique of the "duet" is another means of calling attention to the existential. More than ten fully-developed examples of this highly stylized use of language are scattered through the play. . . . The organization of conversational irregularity into a more rhythmic pattern, the brief return to normal speech, and the merging of variety into unity at the end, which relates so well to the marked tendency of the play to reduce several particulars to one general, are typical of this effort—singularly successful, it seems to me—to transmute the order of everyday reality into a new order of artistic reality. Finally, Beckett uses to his ends language that may be understood on two or more levels. In the climate of *Waiting for Godot*, everything soon begins to be caught up in the oscillation between surface patterns and the universal themes of human existence. . . .

4. The Vacuum, the Existential, and Art

At this stage one might think the artist's task complete. In a sense, however, it is only beginning. For one thing the situation he has created is unstable. Most men are incapable of gazing at the Medusa-head for long. Estragon and Vladimir agree that thought is painful, and we are given a clear idea of the effects of Lucky's "thinking" on Pozzo. It is true that some men, like Perseus, own magic shields, but with long looking the eyes grow dim, and with the fading of what was at first vivid, boredom, or the vacuum, returns. The existential, then, is inadequate to fill the void, and the void, perhaps because it resembles death, is intolerable. Estragon says, "Nothing happens, nobody comes, nobody goes, it's awful!" [p. 27b] He and Vladimir try to do something, anything, in order to "give [them] the impression [they] exist." [p. 44b] The term "pastime" regains all the force of its literal meaning and begins to take on philosophical significance. . . .

At one point they become really rash in their attempts to fill the void and indulge in calisthenics, but Estragon quickly becomes fatigued. Obviously there must be better ways to accomplish their ends. When Pozzo and Lucky are in need of help, assisting them also becomes a way of passing time. It seems that the validity of charity itself is being called into question. At second glance, however, we perceive that where philosophical discussion has led to no practical action and natural sympathy has likewise failed, playing the game in order to fill the void has at least produced results. The scepticism does not seem to be total. If there are few actions in the storehouse, there is no dearth of words. The calisthenics may be of poor quality but the duet that precedes them is quite effective [p. 49a] . . . With enough synonyms almost any pretext, however slight, will serve, for in this case verbal elaboration, sound to fill the silence, is what is needed. It is interesting to note that Estragon usually runs out of synonyms first, while Vladimir may invent a word on occasion. At one point, there is a five-page elaboration of this sort, after which Estragon comments with justifiable pride, "That wasn't such a bad little canter." [p. 42a] Later, when Pozzo has just dropped what is known in some circles as a "conversation stopper," Estragon becomes irritated and says, "Expand! Expand!" [p. 55b] Even the most brutal realities of the human condition can be used as materials for word-play—witness the highly stylized duet on death that extends from page 40a to 41b. Such is the distance of the created pattern from the reality it represents and such is its proximity to the lifeless, fixed form which habit has deprived of its evocative power that it too may serve as a *divertissement*. The mind turns from things to words and sounds, ". . . they whisper. They rustle. They murmur. They rustle." [p. 40b] and formulation has become exorcism.

In this conception of imitation and elaboration in which memory and imagination work together we have obviously come around to considerations of art, its nature and its role. It is clear that all the characters in *Waiting for Godot* are themselves playwrights in embryonic form and that we have many fragmentary plays within Beckett's larger work. . . .

The shifting of the roles of author, characters, and audience, the breaking of the dramatic illusion, as well as the sundry devices for involving the audience in the process of expansion to the existential, all seem to point to the idea that every man is an artist and that life and art are one. We have human existence in the play, and play in human existence. The one gives depth and gravity, the other pleasure and diversion. Here, for example, we see the other face of the comic, which serves not only to destroy patterns but also to fill the void with the laughter of pure enjoyment that eases anguish and relaxes tension. Convention and habit, however, in their stultifying rigidity, are neither good existence nor good art. They form surfaces that mask reality without providing the "occupation, relaxation, recreation" [p. 44b] of art. They, as well as dead art, no doubt,

must constantly be shattered and re-formed. The last scene of
the play reflects this process. Estragon's trousers, which don't
really fit him, fall down when he furnishes Vladimir with the
rope of death, but they are pulled up again as they decide to go
on living. Similarly, Lucky, the performer, causes pain, for he is
a teacher who reveals the hard facts of the human condition.
But Estragon and Vladimir want him to perform again. After
all, he not only thinks; he also dances. And, as we have seen,
the dance may be meaningful and the thought diverting. The
dulce and *utile* of Horace are with us still. . . .

To consider *Waiting for Godot* in terms of art is by no means
to divorce it from life. The dynamic mechanism that informs
the play corresponds to vital movements in human existence,
and each stage represents a response to man's condition. The
complacent bourgeois, traditionally attacked in France by the
artist, remains within the fabric of the given world and takes this
for reality. Those who come to recognize the arbitrary nature of
conventional patterns may recoil into the trap of cynicism,
while some will sink in despair on contact with the void and its
specters. On the difficult way leading toward maturity, however, others will reach the precarious and painful balance
achieved by the true artist, who understands the utility of convention and the necessity of reality. Until the final stage, which
may never materialize, when *divertissement* becomes unnecessary, when Godot either comes or sends better messengers, the
most honest and worthy posture, Beckett seems to suggest, is
perhaps this lucid alternation between illusion and reality, this
anguishing oscillation that is "waiting."

IMAGE AND GODOT

SUE-ELLEN CASE

The structure of *Waiting for Godot* rests upon the relationship between image and action. Image is a paradigm for the play's initial ontology, but action becomes a vehicle of denial, deserting that ontology and finding a new one. The crucial action is the inverse of traditional dramatic progression—it is a backing away. As organizing principles, image and action do not produce theatrical development, but they compose situation, i.e., a locus of relationships.

In the beginning of *Godot*, it is the fusion of abstract and sensual within the image, which is the model both for what is related (content) and how it is related (style). As content, Beckett uses the image's fusion of abstract and sensual to construct the possibility of coupling the experience of existence (the sensual) with an expression of it (the abstract). As style, the image conveys the play's content through its two elements: abstractly, through the use of allusion to various literary, religious, and philosophical systems, and sensually, through the evocation of emotion. Beckett's choice of genre extends this paradigm, for the theater fuses language and gesture, idea and ritual, thus creating itself by both the abstract and the sensual. Play *qua* play then, imitates the image by fusing the same two elements in the same way. This organization constitutes the over-all order of the play as well as the order of each element in the play.

For example, the relation of place to play is not to function as geographic space, nor primarily to ground an event. Place is a structural unit imitative of the image in its gesture to system and in its emotional effect upon the audience. The road gestures to the epic sense and all of the forms that it conjures: journey, trial, and transcendence. Through the epic connotations of the

---

This article was written especially for *Casebook on Waiting for Godot*.

road, the audience experiences certain expectations and waits for them to be fulfilled; but fulfillment is denied. This road leads nowhere, Vladimir and Estragon do not journey upon it, and their trials are not transcended.

The road as structural unit, then, is not the shape of a linear development as in the epic; the stage road couples the possibility of the road as epic journey as its abstract element, with its denial of that expectation as its emotional element. In this way, the two elements of image are the two elements of place— the abstract and the emotional, and their relationship establishes the content of this structural unit. The conceptual unit (that it might be the epic road) establishes the expectation of movement and change, which is denied by the ultimate meaning of road within the play. The gesture is lost. Thus, the way place means is precisely what it means, and place becomes an image of itself.

The place of the play is the road. Upon the road is a small mound, and upon that mound is Estragon, trying to remove his boot. This mound and Estragon's action upon it produce a paradigm for the first movement of the play. Perhaps the mound is Time. Comparable to Clov's "impossible heap" in *Endgame*, or Winnie's envelope in *Happy Days*, the mound of *Godot* is the summit of Estragon's futile, cyclic gestures. The mound and action produce Time as a cumulative succession of cycles. The action is the process of its duration. Here again, the elements of the play function after the model of image. Action provides an experience of Time, which is reinforced by the visual image of the mound as a concept of Time; sensual and abstract interact.

Estragon's action upon the mound is the struggle with his boot. The relationship between Estragon's struggle and his boot also reflects the structure of image. The boot is too small and hurts his foot. Estragon struggles to remove it, but the boot will not budge. This action refutes an existential interpretation of Beckett's characters. Estragon does not define himself and the world, but is defined by his world. His desire and frustration are both produced by the boot. It is the boot which marks the limits of his action.

The boot and its strict size are the order of existence, the doorway to experience; they call upon Estragon to act, but he can have no real effect upon them. They are his, and he is stuck with them. They do not fit his feet in either act. The need for action is invoked by them, and the meaning of action resides in them. The boot is the visual limit of Estragon's foot and the experiential limit of his action. Conceptually, it is the external world as the limit of self; experientially, it is the process of being limited. All of Estragon's action is circumscribed. Later he attempts to leave the stage, but is forced back on both sides by hostile groups. Like his action, Estragon himself is circumscribed. His role is a result of external forces, and not of his own creation. The character literally reaches his limits. Thus, this particular condition of Estragon is determined by the nature of his world, and his action is prescribed by it. Ontology, then, determines experience. The condition of the character is determined, not existential.

Not only does Estragon reach the limits of self, but self is the limit of Estragon. This becomes dramatically evident in the relationship of Vladimir and Estragon. They couple the abstract and sensual as mirrors, reflecting one another's condition. This is the only possible relationship between these confined, cyclic personalities, for anything else might cause development, or establish cause and effect. Vladimir's hat is a mirror of Estragon's boot; Vladimir's attempt to understand the discrepancy among the gospels is Estragon's attempt to remove his boot, and so on. It becomes evident that their relationship is another reflection of the organization of the image; the emotional and conceptual worlds are fused by reflecting one another. The way they mean is what they mean. Thus, the bi-cyclic relationship, like place and circumstance, uses the model of the image for its meaning, its ontology, and its determinant of action and interaction.

Since all is subject to this ontology, the only condition left to the characters is to submit. Knowledge is submission: it is awaited ("Let's wait and see what he says . . . till we know exactly how we stand") or it is remembered ("what exactly did we ask him for?"). Even the assessment of one's own condition is either given or denied. To passive creatures submissive to this ontology, it is not a role that is important ("Where do we come in?"), but a condition ("On our hands and knees."). Yet it is role which will be the catalyst for the denial of the ontology.

The first act begins with Estragon struggling with his boot. In the second act the boots stand empty while Vladimir sings and reflects. These two opening scenes summarize the movement of the play. At first, existence and meaning are coupled— Estragon struggles against the boot, is seriously involved in the process. By the second act, Vladimir broods upon and sings the endless cycle of existence; he captures it in a form. This chasm between man experiencing and man thinking about experience already exists in the first act ("No use wriggling. The essential doesn't change."), but gapes wide with the entrance of Pozzo and Lucky, who make role manifest on stage. Whether Pozzo and Lucky are variants of the roles of Vladimir and Estragon, or play independent roles observable to the friends, the effect is the same: Vladimir and Estragon can step back to observe expression and identity confined to roles. Pozzo's play within a play serves to manifest the role of self by expressing the agony of himself, then stepping back from that expression: "There wasn't a word of truth in it." In relation to Pozzo, Vladimir and Estragon portray the process of consciousness encountering its subject matter—Pozzo's expression of condition as role. However, since Pozzo's statement is an inadequate expression of all of consciousness, they reject that statement as a reflection of consciousness. Subject matter and its context of meaning no longer fuse with the experience of existence.

When Pozzo rises to his highest images (associating Lucky with angel and crucifix), the drama shows the failure of imagery. Vladimir and Estragon undermine Pozzo's context, reducing his statements about existence to mere entertainment: "The circus . . . the music-hall." The apocalyptic is diminished to the obscene by Vladimir's exit to piss.

acteristic position and are seated on the low mound. Although Vladimir initially assumes a proprietary air as Estragon's protector in this first act, it is Estragon who dominates, forcing Vladimir into suffering at the uncertainty of the time and place, or probability of the appointment with Godot. Despite despair at the "horror of his situation," Estragon assumes the power of choice: to leave, part, hang himself. Vladimir, however, assumes no possible choice: they must wait for Godot. It is only when Vladimir denies Estragon's claim to freedom—"his prerogatives" and "rights"—by insisting, "We got rid of them," that he forces Estragon into suffering and the first climactic moment of frozen passion in the play: "*Silence. They remain motionless, arms dangling, heads sunk, sagging at the knees.*" [p. 13b]

Just before the entrance of Pozzo and Lucky, Estragon repeatedly asks whether or not they are "tied" to Godot. "To Godot?" Vladimir answers. "Tied to Godot! What an idea! No question of it. (*Pause.*) For the moment." [p. 14b] A moment later, Lucky enters, tied "by means of a rope passed round his neck" to Pozzo who commands, rope-end in one hand, a whip in the other. The analogue of the achieved Pozzo-Lucky relationship to Vladimir's longed-for relationship to Godot offers an appalling perspective. For if Pozzo is, as he claims, "made in God's image," then so much the worse for God, let alone Godot. A posturing, pretentious, hammy, petulant, bombastic bully, Pozzo is very much like his name (a "well" in Italian)— vertical space; a dark hole that requires filling; a shaft of emptiness that might lead to water, but more likely to gas: empty space in the shape of a man—as easily deflated as inflated.

Tied by choice to Pozzo, Lucky merits the names he is called: pig, hog, slave, carrier, creature, misery, scum, etc. Once he was Pozzo's "knook" (jester) and "good angel," "so kind . . . helpful . . . and entertaining," a dancer who "capered. For joy"; "He even used to think very prettily once" and taught Pozzo "Beauty, grace, truth of the first water." As Pozzo observes, "But for him all my thoughts, all my feelings, would have been of common things." [p. 22b] But Lucky is not only the teacher-creator of Pozzo, his tyrant-master, but also of himself, the slave-servant. "Remark that I might just as well have been in his shoes and he in mine," [p. 21b] Pozzo remarks, and then puns on Lucky-chance: "If chance had not willed otherwise." Now Lucky is by choice, out of fear, the slave who hopes to please through the extremity of his suffering, the Carrier who, because he insists upon his burdens, can be contemptuously likened to Atlas, the first and ultimate Carrier, the scapegoat of creation, who was forced by Jupiter to his perpetual task. Lucky is the figure of all the destructive relationships insisted upon by man: slaves who perpetuate their tyrants; artists and thinkers who insist upon serving vulgar appetites; all men who create harsh, demeaning and ultimately meaningless gods.

At the climax of the scene (and turning point of the play) Lucky dances and thinks on command. With these performances, Lucky provides a central metaphor for *Godot* and modern man. He calls his dance "The Net." Pozzo says, "He thinks he's entangled in a net." [p. 27a] With this reference the play rejects any exclusively Christian interpretation, for "The Net" finds no place in the New Testament cosmology; it does appear, however, in most pre-Christian cosmologies and is usually associated with the retributive power of older, harsher gods. The Old Testament Yahweh; the Sumerian gods, Tammuz and Shamash; the Hindu god, Varuna; the early Greek sky gods—all are Gods of the Net. "My net also will I spread upon him," says Yahweh of a rebellious prince of Israel, "and he shall be taken in my snare." [Ezekiel 12:12] As late as the tragedies, the Greek gods were associated with the Net. In *Agamemnon*, Zeus is depicted as snaring Troy in a bloody net. As the shadows of his fate begin to press close, Oedipus cries out, "Ah, what net has God been weaving for me?" The implication is that Lucky (like Troy and Oedipus) is entangled in the Net of his own weaving, and hence is the servant of an indifferently just god.

But in the East the Net is a figure for the cosmos—the "Net of Heaven." And the Nothing that Beckett's plays finally affirm is much closer to the Nothing that is Brahma or Tao than to the elaborate Something that is the enthroned Christian God. Lao-tzu's verses (*Tao Te Ching*, LXXIII) might serve as an epigraph for *Godot*:

> *Heaven hates what it hates,*
> *Who knows the reason why?*
> *Therefore even the sage treats some things as difficult.*
> *The way of heaven*
> > *Excels in overcoming though it does not contend,*
> > *In responding though it does not speak,*
> > *In attracting though it does not summon,*
> > *In laying plans though it appears slack.*
> *The net of heaven is cast wide. Though the mesh is not fine,*
> > *yet nothing ever slips through.*

Even by suicide.

Lucky's shuffling, panting, constricted dance is thus an enactment of the self-determined fate of all the players: entanglement in the Net. His "thinking" is an imitation of the same action, a brilliant verbal demonstration [pp. 28b–29b] of man's entanglement in uncertainties ("for reasons unknown") that cannot be certainly claimed ("but time will tell"); the mad contradictions of irrational belief ("a personal God . . . with white beard . . . outside time without extension who from the heights of divine apathia"); the equally mad contradictions of rational belief ("as a result of the labors left unfinished . . . it is established beyond all doubt"); and the mad assertive and qualifying fragments of language with which man tries to patch together the impossibilities of his discourse ("considering what is more," "the facts are there," "in short," "in brief," "in spite of," etc.), but which finally serve only to glut and stifle mouth, ear, and mind.

But the "thinking" makes its own kind of sense. Lucky's unfinished labor of thought is composed of three long complicated dependent clauses that never resolve in a completing, confirming main clause, but instead (despite Lucky's labors) tumble into a disintegration of all structure, an unending tangle of words. And in its tortuous suspension that can find no release, Lucky's monologue also accomplishes an imitation of helpless, doomed entanglement in the Net. But since the linked subjects of the three clauses are three possible dooms for man, form and matter are joined and give voice to each other. Each long clause promises disintegration, swift or slow: the firing of the firmament, the blasting of hell to heaven; "and considering what is more," the wasting, pining, shrinking, fading away of man; "and considering what is more much more grave," the fiery death of the sun and consequent doom of the earth and its life, "running water running fire . . . the great cold the great dark . . . the earth abode of stones." With this embodiment of the Net, and prophecy of man's possibly probable end, Lucky becomes the talisman that his name suggests, the figure of magic and symbol, oracle and taboo, the mind as well as flesh become a scapegoat for all men's unfinished creation—and, hence, the mind gone mad.

In Act II, the world has gone mad. All is intensified and accelerated. While Act I can be played for laughs, Act II shrieks. The tree has burst into leaf overnight. The players move feverishly about the stage or sprawl in chaos. Nothing makes any sense; all is fragmented and absurd. Act II plunges into the gasping spilling of the ending section of Lucky's speech. Vladimir longs for Lucky's madness, the final entanglement in the Net, and would drag Estragon with him—playing the Pozzo-Lucky game. At last, wearing Lucky's hat, Vladimir enunciates the madness he longs for: while Pozzo cries for help, a noble and inappropriate rhetoric blooms in Vladimir's mouth.

While Vladimir is "happy," intoxicated by the signs of change, Estragon grimly observes, "It's never the same pus from one second to the next" [p. 39a]—echoing Clytemnestra's view of the grim necessity of their cursed lives that drove her to net Agamemnon and that would continue its course: "Before the old sore heals, new pus collects." (Louis MacNeice translation.) Finally, Estragon flees the awful game, but is driven back, trapped by others: "They're coming!" he shouts. "I'm in hell!"

[p. 47b] And he gives up, saying himself what had been Vladimir's insistence, "I'm waiting for Godot," and in a pitch of compression of desire, resistance, and despair, summing up all the mechanical horror of their condition, "Let's go. We can't. Ah!" [p. 50a]

The horror of the situation extends explicitly to the audience in this second act. They are referred to as "these corpses," "these skeletons," "A charnel-house!", "not a soul in sight." They are the "dead voices" of the living dead, the bog in which the two tramps must endure a waiting. Near the end, when Vladimir soliloquizes while Estragon sleeps, his perceptions of the Net entangle the audience as certainly as the players: "The air is full of our cries. [. . .] But habit is a great deadener. [. . .] At me too someone is looking, of me too someone is saying, He is sleeping, he knows nothing, let him sleep on. (*Pause.*) I can't go on! (*Pause.*) What have I said?" [pp. 58a–58b]

But despite his perceptions, he goes on; for here in Act II, Vladimir dominates as Estragon dominated Act I. Act II opens with Vladimir's song of death and endless repetition. The play closes with the two tramps assuming Vladimir's characteristic pose, standing before the tree, uttering the litany that closes their nightly performance—"Well? Shall we go? / Yes, let's go."—and not moving.

Although the ending is ceremonious, a ritual that repeats almost exactly the ending of the evening before, there is on this night a significant difference. Vladimir goes on, and carries Estragon with him, by choice; he knows now that Godot will not come, but chooses to go on for want of anything else the mind can conceive to do.

What he has elected is hell, a self-entanglement in a self-woven net. The bleak landscape of their existence is contained within a cosmos of old and indifferent gods whose ultimate necessity expresses Nothing. Within this bleak indifference man weaves a net of damnation from strands of Christianity become trivial—the hope of salvation by a ridiculous conception of a little God with a white beard who "if we dropped Him" would "punish us." The pathos in the travesty is the figure of Estragon, the victim, again standing barefoot like Christ: man's flesh crucified by his deadly mind.

CYCLICAL DRAMATURGY

LUDOVIC JANVIER

The identity of Godot is one of the least important things in Waiting for Godot. Beckett was quite right to reply, when asked what Godot meant: "If I had known, I would have said so in the play."

Though Vladimir and Estragon wait for Godot, each of their words and gestures reaches far beyond that proper noun, which is so irritating to critics who wish to look outside the play, and who cast their eyes toward nothing. Godot is a name for nothing; it is nothing; or as Estragon says in the line that summarizes the whole play: "We always find something, eh Didi, to give us the impression we exist?" [p. 44a]

Godot is the name for waiting, and that waiting unfolds in immutable space—except for five leaves on the tree that designates the bare place where the characters remain. Thus, space becomes a metaphor for repetitive time, and time imposes itself as the only respiratory dimension. Vladimir and Estragon refer to the environment in which they live their difficult present, only by that signal which punctuates the void of their time; it is no accident that the signal takes the form of a refrain: "We're waiting for Godot," dividing the flow of time into

From Pour Samuel Beckett (Paris: Les Editions de Minuit, 1966), copyright © 1966 by Les Editions de Minuit. Reprinted by permission of Georges Borchardt. Translated from the French by Ruby Cohn.

repetitive periods of waiting, into comparable fragments of immutability, all stemming from the reference to an *a priori:* Godot, the time of living. The idea of refrain, or repetition, is seen in several details, and it is the focal point of the entire structure, for the "dramaturgy" of the play is cyclical.

Cycle of "Days"

What is done that is not redone in Godot? What is said that is not resaid? It is no use telling us that the second cycle of the play is actually the next day; the new day is not a new day, for Beckett specifies that it is the *same* time, *same* place, and *same* light, and the day will be punctuated by the *same* moments as the day before. Tomorrow, yesterday, have only as much sense as the question that Vladimir and Estragon ask themselves: "What did we do yesterday?" Implied is complete doubt about traces of the past.

Cycle of Characters

If their childish and confusing questions can disorient us toward the duration of time, and can situate these repetitions in totally new beginnings that threaten sanity itself, do not the Pozzo-Lucky couple contradict this temporal dis-indication? They reappear at the right time of the second day, but they reappear changed: Pozzo is blind, and at Lucky's mercy. He is still cruel, but he falls, and is beginning to collapse. . . . In short, Pozzo incarnates time. But simultaneously, he explodes the conception of himself as a point of reference; it is no accident that of all the characters, Pozzo has most to say about time. With Vladimir and Estragon, we think that we can point to yesterday as the last time Pozzo could still see, but he tells us: "I woke up one fine day as blind as Fortune." [p. 55b] And to Vladimir, who still believes in yesterday: "Don't question me! The blind have no notion of time." Pozzo refuses to admit that he was there yesterday. What oracle speaks through Pozzo's mouth, if not the immutable present, which never ends, which is always beginning, and from which one cannot escape? . . .

In contrast to Beckett's novels, the play's lived action is converted into a present. Instead of speaking about it, it does the speaking. Instead of aiming at it, it lets itself speak and thus reveals its overwhelming quality; the present is seen as an immense womb in which human existence is played out, without leaps or returns. In sacrificing intimacy for totality, in surrounding man rather than reaching his depths, the drama brings us closer to him, or at least gives us a more complete view of him.

Cycle of Actions, Gestures, Words

The same questioning pulsations cut these similar days into identical moments: "Nothing to be done." "Let's play this or that." "What are we doing here?" (Answer: "We're waiting for Godot.") "If we parted?" And the two days end with the same ritual phrases that testify not only to the inability to leave but above all to the eternal repetition of that inability. "Well? Shall we go?" asks Estragon, and Vladimir answers: "Yes, let's go." But of course they do not move. And the second time, Vladimir asks the question, and Estragon replies. But of course, they move no more than the first time. In this inverted binary structure, which exhausts their possibilities, we have proof of the perfect circularity of time. Nothing ever finishes, and everything begins again.

This can also be seen in the structure of the dialogue, which is full of echoes. Estragon and Vladimir use language as tennis players use a ball. Examples are so numerous that the whole play is minted in echoes. . . . Through such exchanges, Vladimir and Estragon have the illusion of progressing through a thick immutability, which is their life. Pozzo is of some help with his blustering verbiage, laden with aphorisms and pitiable outbursts; progressive banality installs its labyrinth of phrases. Lucky's speech is distinctive, for its disorder is expressed by mechanical repetition—the broken record of time.

Thus, nothing escapes from time. The characters are in a hollow, from which they speak the stagnation that they live, the nothing-to-be-done. Time and space have always been what the character measures and sees, here and now; the latter points to the eternity of the former, and between them man is trapped, forced into an admission of progress, or memory, or discovery, or recognition. "Recognize!" a furious Estragon exclaims to Vladimir, who has urged him to recollect that they were there yesterday. "What is there to recognize? . . ." [p. 39b] Nothing can provide an escape from the eternal instant grasped simultaneously by body and mind, whenever they move toward awareness. I am inscribed in time; therefore I can never do anything else than measure this moment which is always new when I think in terms of time, and yet each time I agree to the proof of time passing.

Since Estragon and Vladimir, Lucky and Pozzo, tell us the time that it has always been, this might be a despairing witness, and yet it is the most banal affirmation; these outbursts in which they denounce their eternal momentary condition, scarcely disturb their existence *à deux* or *à quatre*, imposed upon bodies by time. Fraternal bodies, fraternal to one another and to us, because they have a quality of presence, as Alain Robbe-Grillet noticed, a weight of being there, which pushes into the background the ideas that they incarnate.

They both confess that there is "nothing to be done"; it is as a couple that they traverse immutable space-time into an eternity which summarizes being-there in gestures and words of complicity and habit. In *Waiting for Godot*, more than any other work, we are aware that there is no other solution to the difficulty of being, but the individual-couple. This existence-game in couples has two faces: Vladimir-Estragon in light, Pozzo-Lucky in shadow, and it is of some interest to see how each couple penetrates the other with nuances.

Vladimir and Estragon love one another, but sometimes they cannot stand one another; one's odor irritates the other; one affirms that the other sleeps and pisses better without him; the couple exists so well as a couple that they periodically wonder whether to continue together and even imagine a separation; only to admit coldly, with some bitterness and unexpressed joy, that separation is impossible. Cruel moments, enduring love.

In contrast, Pozzo and Lucky represent the executioner and his victim, the master and slave. The one is brutalized by the other's cruelty, but habituated to it, like an animal, and probably he even seeks it, because that is what gives him life. The other sadistically exercises an exhausting domination which tires him too, and leaves him in a moral solitude that we may condemn. And yet that condemnation will turn upon itself when we see Pozzo in Act II, still bound to Lucky, but blind, still vicious but weeping, still a master of rhetoric but less striking, and soon struck by Vladimir and Estragon, weaklings and strangers. Pozzo is a curious character, an eloquent executioner and amateur of blue skies; with his victim Lucky, he forms another fraternal couple, combining detestable viciousness and the need for tenderness, so that this couple is finally not unattractive, mechanical though they seem, and alienated when compared with Vladimir and Estragon. Pozzo, a kind of storyteller, has invented his creature, Lucky, as the voices in Beckett's novels invent. . . . Pozzo and Lucky, the evil ones, implicitly criticize Vladimir and Estragon, the good ones. One couple criticizes the other, and prevents us from sentimentalizing. . . .

Waiting for Godot is an "action" in which tenderness and cruelty, light and shadow, balance each other, and share this immutable space-time which is the human zone. Four states of collapse, in perpetual movement, meet on a bare surface.

The tone makes an optimistic tragedy of this non-drama. Vladimir and Estragon are unhappy; Pozzo and Lucky are also unhappy at being there; these four beings turn and return in this prison-space; they come and go in this cage of time; they speak and forget, speak and endure, make gestures to feel alive; they know, and feel that everything is useless. But they are not sad. *Waiting for Godot* is not hell; it is a neutral place, and there is even a certain happiness in the blackest of their abandonment, in what should be felt as dark, but which is only the totality of the human condition. In Beckett's novels, the immediacy of the narrating voice prevented us from recognizing a brother, because he was damned. But theatrical distance saves the writer from silence, the work from madness, and it permits us to see those who speak; they are men like us. Speaking calmly of their misery, and feeling that they represent human banality, these characters reveal a concentrated portrait of our own misery, of our own banality. Tender tramps and boy-scout outcasts, sadistic master and reified servant, speak to us calmly about ourselves. And it is this calm which saves them from passion and avoids tragedy for them, plunging them into the immutability of eternity. They do not kill each other, they weep moderately, they converse in little jokes, they still move slightly; they are men who endure, at their ease in the worst that can happen. *Waiting for Godot,* or courage.

BECKETT'S CLOWNS

GENEVIÈVE SERREAU

Vladimir and Estragon suggest clowns more than they do tramps: Footit and Chocolat, Alex and Zavetta, Pipo and Rhum, the Fratellini trio, the Marx brothers, or the traditional comedians of English music hall. Clowns are second-degree characters who have a precise stage function, resembling that of the Shakespearean fool. One does not ask questions about their origin, social condition, or language—which is alternately coarse, poetic, and profound—just as one does not ask these questions about the Fool of *Lear,* about Touchstone or Thersites.

The text of *Godot* and its scenic directions re-enforce these clown suggestions: derbies for all characters; the spectacular entrance of Pozzo and Lucky, the latter using a whip like a

From *Histoire du Nouveau Théâtre* (Paris: Editions Gallimard, 1966), copyright © 1966 by Editions Gallimard. Reprinted by permission. Translated from the French by Ruby Cohn.

circus animal-trainer; Pozzo's generous offer of Lucky's burlesque recitatif as a dependable entertainment that has stood
the test of time. Or the hat pantomime (three hats for two
heads) which Gogo and Didi enact with the seriousness of acro-
batic jugglers; or the slapstick fall of all four actors piled up on
one another.

Vladimir points out: "Worse than the pantomime." "The
circus," corrects Estragon. Vladimir: "The music-hall." But
Estragon insists, "The circus." [p. 23b] In the circus, clowns
traditionally play a parodic role, one of demystification. During
the heyday of Sarah Bernhardt, Footit did a grotesque parody
of the great actress in Cleopatra's deathbed scene. But in *Godot*
the sacred monster that must be demystified is man. *Waiting
for Godot* parodies a situation which is suddenly revealed in
all its nakedness—man thrown into existence and seeking to
solve his own problem, or rather renouncing any solution since
he cannot use his traditional tools (reality of space, time, and
matter). What is happening—that "Nothing is happening"—
is absence, and at the heart of the absence is a wait for something, someone, which will give everything a meaning. That is
what it means to be saved. Saved from the absurd. Saved from
the fate of a life which one can neither live nor die, which is
endless while it lasts, and which can only be ridiculed. Vladimir
affirms this at the end of the play: If Godot comes, "we'll be
saved." And at the beginning of the play, the first theme is
that of the two thieves crucified with Christ, one of whom is
saved in the Gospel of Luke. "It's a reasonable percentage,"
declares Vladimir, who is nevertheless uneasy about a grace
which falls on one and neglects the other, as it may divide the
Gogo-Didi couple.

All through the play, Vladimir will suggest other themes in
order to keep the play going—the play that is always on the
point of dying but that cannot die—like life itself—the play in
which words, as irreplaceable as blood, remain the last resort
and the last courage.

"We're inexhaustible," notes Vladimir. And Estragon: "We
always find something, eh Didi, to give us the impression we

exist?" In the dialogues of professional clowns, the ball is kept rolling by differences of temperament or of profession, clearly indicated from the beginning; thus the first *zanni* of the *commedia dell'arte* is petulant and active, and the second is horrified and passive; this is the traditional contrast between the white clown and Auguste (played by François and Albert Fratellini). The most trivial theme provokes contrasting reactions from the two clowns; and this very misunderstanding, this distance, causes the theme to advance, ricochet, bounce, and take on new meaning from the games, *quiproquos*, and *lazzi*. The spectacle is pure play, pure movement of a parodic action which propagates itself, giving rise to laughter, without any other apparent necessity than the pleasure of continuing. Whenever the mechanism seems to grind, where it seems to have free "play," play is established. Although the contrast between Gogo and Didi is attenuated, it is still strong enough to move the various themes forward. Several sequences depend upon Estragon's lack of memory and Vladimir's constant attempts to resituate himself in time and space. Especially those lines which refer to the place, time, and purpose of their appointment with Godot. Gogo systematically doubts; he is totally immersed in a kind of nightmare of nothingness in which everything = everything (nothing = nothing), and he thus erodes the few striking certainties to which Didi clings; thus, the sequence of dialogue consumes itself for lack of contradiction, and the risk reappears that everything will sink into silence, into annihilation. . . .

Several times, Vladimir complains of his partner's sluggishness: "Come on, Gogo, return the ball, can't you, once in a way?" The whole play takes its rhythm from these moments when a sequence has been completed and everything returns to zero for an instant—a dizzy moment of void, all language spent—then quickly, urgently, one or the other brings new words into play, starts the word-machine again, exists. This is what binds them irrevocably to one another, even more deeply than their common wait for Godot; this, and the way each has become a habit for the other, with his individual miseries—

that inexpressible depth of old ruminated unhappiness. Even fragile, half-forgotten, and constantly questioned, these memories are the soil in which all Beckett's couples take root. The Didi-Gogo couple has miraculously preserved tenderness, a solicitude that never becomes aggressive; a kind of desperate compassion bathes the nameless desert of human relations.

Everything is play in *Godot*. Like the movements of a drowning man who tries to save his breath and his life while struggling between two waves, the play of Gogo and Didi is all that separates them from nothingness; it is their only weapon against the void, enabling them to bear the unbearable wait; this ludicrous activity is intensely vital. This is what gives the "Nothing happens" of *Godot* its incomparable density, its urgency, its necessary rhythm and pace, comparable to certain of Bach's fugues.

Even though Gogo and Didi are terrified of the Pozzo-Lucky couple, their entrance is a godsend, since the burden of entertainment will no longer fall on them alone. This perpetual entertainment (in Pascal's sense of *divertissement*) which is their lot, is a ridiculous parody of human existence, and they are both aware that it is parody and that it is ridiculous. They are therefore tempted to parody the parody, to detach themselves from this absurd dream in which they move, speak, suffer, and wait, in order to play at being Didi and Gogo in the process of moving, speaking, suffering, and waiting (or perhaps to play at Beckett in the process of writing *Godot*). One of the surest sources of comedy in *Godot* is this reflection of themselves in their own consciousness, this separation from themselves in a situation that is doubly ridiculous.

"I begin to weary of this motif," says Vladimir. Estragon proposes, "That's the idea, let's ask each other questions." [p. 41b] After a particularly trivial discussion of radishes and carrots, Vladimir remarks: "This is becoming really insignificant." [p. 44a] Since that is exactly what the average member of the audience is thinking, the barb hits him directly, but Gogo's savage answer follows immediately, coarsely suggesting a kind of tragic dimension: "Not enough."

As at the circus or the music hall, the spectator is involved in this process of detachment; what happens repetitively is that after a sudden destruction of theatrical illusion, the stage becomes a stage, that bounded cube which opens only into the terrifying gulf of the audience. Thus, Vladimir cries out to a frightened Gogo, who "makes a rush towards back": "Imbecile! There's no way out there." Then, gesturing toward the audience: "There! Not a soul in sight! Off you go! Quick! (*He pushes Estragon towards auditorium. Estragon recoils in horror.*) You won't? (*He contemplates auditorium.*) Well I can understand that." [p. 47b]

These lines always arouse laughter, even from the most restive members of the audience; so do the lines in which Didi and Gogo comment on their situation as it is reduced to stage time and place: "Charming evening we're having." "Unforgettable." "In the meantime nothing happens." The impatient spectator on the point of walking out, stops, for the author has suddenly become an accomplice in his own confusion through Pozzo's question: "You find it tedious?" and Vladimir's answer: "I've been better entertained." [p. 26a]

THERE'S LOTS OF TIME IN *GODOT*
RICHARD SCHECHNER

Two duets and a false solo, that's *Waiting for Godot*. Its structure is more musical than dramatic, more theatrical than literary. The mode is pure performance: song and dance, music-hall routine, games. And the form is a spinning away, a centrifugal wheel in which the center—Time—can barely hold the

From *Modern Drama*, December, 1966. Reprinted by permission.

parts, Gogo and Didi, Pozzo and Lucky, the Boy(s). The characters arrive and depart in pairs, and when they are alone they
are afraid: half of them is gone. The Boy isn't really by himself,
though one actor plays the role(s). "It wasn't you came yesterday," states Vladimir in Act II. "No Sir," the Boy says. "This is
your first time." "Yes Sir." [p. 58b] Only Godot is alone, at the
center of the play and all outside it at once. "What does he do,
Mr. Godot? . . . He does nothing, Sir." [p. 59a] But even Godot
is linked to Gogo/Didi. "To Godot? Tied to Godot! What an
idea! No question of it. (*Pause.*) For the moment." [p. 14b]
Godot is also linked to the Boy(s), who tend his sheep and
goats, who are his messengers. Nor can we forget that Godot
cares enough for Gogo/Didi to send someone each night to tell
them the appointment will not be kept. What exquisite politeness.

Pozzo (and we must assume, Lucky) has never heard of
Godot, although the promised meeting is to take place on his
land. Pozzo is insulted that *his* name means nothing to
Gogo/Didi. "We're not from these parts," Estragon says in
apology, and Pozzo deigns, "You are human beings none the
less." [p. 15b] Pozzo/Lucky have no appointment to keep.
Despite the cracking whip and Pozzo's air of big business on the
make, their movements are random, to and fro across the land,
burdens in hand, rope in place: there is always time to stop and
proclaim. In Act I, after many adieus, Pozzo says, "I don't seem
to be able . . . (*long hesitation*) . . . to depart." And when he
does move, he confesses, "I need a running start." In Act II,
remembering nothing about "yesterday," Pozzo replies to
Vladimir's question, "Where do you go from here," with a
simple. "On." It is Pozzo's last word.

The Pozzo/Lucky duet is made of improvised movements
and set speeches (Lucky's has run down). The Gogo/Didi duet
is made of set movements (they must be at this place each
night at dusk to wait for Godot to come or night to fall) and
improvised routines spun out of long-ago learned habits. Pozzo
who starts in no place is worried only about Time; he ends
without time but with a desperate need to move. Gogo-Didi

are "tied" to this place and want only for time to pass. Thus, part way through the first act the basic scenic rhythm of *Godot* is established by the strategic arrangement of characters: Gogo/ Didi (and later the Boy) have definite appointments, a rendez- vous they *must* keep. Pozzo/Lucky are free agents, aimless, not tied to anything but each other. For this reason, Pozzo's watch is very important to him. Having nowhere to go, his only rela- tion to the world is in knowing "the time." The play is a confrontation between the rhythms of place and time. Ulti- mately they are coordinates of the same function.

Of course, Pozzo's freedom is illusory. He is tied to Lucky— and vice versa—as tightly as the others are tied to Godot and the land. In the scenic calculus of the play, rope = appoint- ment. As one coordinate weakens, the other tightens. Thus, when Pozzo/Lucky lose their sense of time, there is a cor- responding increase in their need to cover space. Lucky's speech is imperfect memory, an uncontrollable stream of unconscious- ness, while Pozzo's talk is all *tirade*, a series of set speeches, learned long ago, and slowly deserting the master actor, just as the things which define his identity—watch, pipe, atomizer— desert him. I am reminded of Yeats' *Circus Animals' Desertion* where images fail the old poet who is finally forced to "lie down where all the ladders start/ In the foul rag-and-bone shop of the heart." Here, too, Pozzo will find himself (Lucky is already there). Thus we see these two in their respective penultimate phases, comforted only by broken bursts of eloquence, laments for that lost love, clock time.

The pairing of characters—those duets—links time and space, presents them as discontinuous coordinates. Gogo/Didi are not sure whether the place in Act II is the same as that in Act I; Pozzo cannot remember yesterday; Gogo/Didi do not recall what they did yesterday. "We should have thought of it [suicide] a million years ago, in the nineties." Gogo either for- gets at once, or he never forgets. This peculiar sense of time and place is not centered *in* the characters, but *between* them. Just as it takes two lines to fix a point in space, so it takes two characters to *unfix* our normal expectations of time, place, and being. This pairing is not unique to *Waiting for Godot;* it is a favorite device of contemporary playwrights. The Pupil and the Professor in *The Lesson,* Claire and Solange in *The Maids,* Peter and Jerry in *The Zoo Story:* these are of the same species as *Godot.* What might these duets mean or be? Each of them suggests a precarious existence, of sense of self and self-in-the-world so dependent on "the other" as to be inextricably bound up in the other's physical presence. In these plays "experience" is not "had" by a single character, but "shared" between them. It is not a question of fulfillment—of why Romeo wants Juliet—but of existence. By casting the characters homosexually, the author removes the "romantic" element: these couples are not joined because of some biological urge but because of some metaphysical necessity. The drama that emerges from such pairing is intense and locked-in—a drama whose focus is internal without being "psychological." Internalization without psychology is naked drama, theater unmediated by character. That is why, in these plays, the generic structure of their elements—farce, melodrama, vaudeville—is so unmistakably clear. There is no way (or need) to hide structure: that's all there is. But still, in *Godot,* there are meaningful differences between Vladimir and Estragon, Pozzo and Lucky; but even these shadings of individuation are seen only through the couple: to know one character, you have to know both.

In Aristotelian terms drama is made of the linked chain: action > plot > character > thought. Connections run efficiently in either direction, although for the most part one seeks the heart of a play in its action (as Fergusson uses that term). These same elements are in *Godot,* but the links are broken. The discontinuity of time is reflected on this more abstract level of structure. Thus what Gogo and Didi do is not what they are thinking; nor can we understand their characters by adding and relating events to thoughts. And the action of the play—waiting—is not what they are after but what they want most to avoid. What, after all, are their games for? They wish to "fill time" in such a way that the vessel "containing" their activities is unnoticed amid the activities themselves. Whenever there is nothing "to do" they remember why they are here: To wait for Godot. That memory, that direct confrontation with Time, is painful. They play, invent, move, sing to avoid the sense of waiting. Their *activities* are therefore keeping them from a consciousness of the *action* of the play. Although there is a real change in Vladimir's understanding of his experience (he learns precisely what "nothing to be done" means) and in Pozzo's life, these changes and insights do not emerge from the plot (as Lear's "wheel of fire" does), but stand outside of what's happened. Vladimir has his epiphany while Estragon sleeps—in a real way his perception is a function of the sleeping Gogo. Pozzo's understanding, like the man himself, is blind. Structurally as well as thematically, *Godot* is an "incompleted" play; and its openness is not at the end (as *The Lesson* is open-ended) but in many places throughout: it is a play of gaps and pauses, of broken-off dialogue, of speech and action turning into time-avoiding games and routines. Unlike Beckett's perfectly modulated *Molloy*, *Waiting for Godot* is designed off-balance. It is the very opposite of *Oedipus*. In *Godot* we do not have the meshed ironies of experience, but that special anxiety associated with question marks preceded and followed by nothing.

What then holds *Godot* together? Time, habit, memory, and games form the texture of the play and provide both its literary and theatrical interest. In *Proust*, Beckett speaks of habit and memory in a way that helps us understand *Godot*:

> The laws of memory are subject to the more general laws of habit. Habit is a compromise effected between the individual and his environment, or between the individual and his own organic eccentricities, the guarantee of a dull inviolability, the lightning-conductor of his existence. Habit is the ballast that chains the dog to his vomit. . . . Life is a succession of habits, since the individual is a succession of individuals. . . . The creation of the world did not take place once and for all, but takes place every day.

The other side of "dull inviolability" is "knowing," and it is this that Gogo/Didi must avoid if they are to continue. But knowledge is precisely what Didi has near the end of the play. It ruins everything for him:

> Was I sleeping, while the others suffered? Am I sleeping now? To-morrow, when I wake, or think I do, what shall I say of to-day? That with Estragon my friend, at this place, until the fall of night, I waited for Godot? That Pozzo passed, with his carrier, and that he spoke to us? Probably. But in all that what truth will there be? [Looking at Estragon] He'll know nothing. He'll tell me about the blows he received and I'll give him a carrot.   [p. 58a]

Then, paraphrasing Pozzo, Didi continues:

> Astride of a grave and a difficult birth. Down in the hole, lingeringly, the grave-digger puts on the forceps. We have time to grow old. The air is full of our cries. (He listens.) But habit is a great deadener. (He looks again at Estragon.) At me too someone is looking, of me too someone is saying, He is sleeping, he knows nothing, let him sleep on. (Pause.) I can't go on! (Pause.) What have I said?

In realizing that he knows nothing, in seeing that habit is the great deadener—in achieving an ironic point of view toward himself, Didi knows everything, and wishes he did not. For him Pozzo's single instant has become "lingeringly." For Pozzo "the same day, the same second" is enough to enfold all human experience; Didi realizes that there is "time to grow old." But habit will rescue him. Having shouted his anger, frustration, helplessness ("I can't go on!"), Didi is no longer certain of what he said. Dull inviolability has been violated, but only for an instant: one instant is enough for insight, and we have a lifetime to forget. The Boy enters. Unlike the first act, Didi asks him no questions. Instead Didi makes statements. "He won't come this evening. . . . But he'll come to-morrow." For the first time, Didi asks the Boy about Godot. "What does he do, Mr. Godot? . . . Has he a beard, Mr. Godot?" The Boy answers: Godot does nothing, the beard is probably white. Didi says—after a silence—"Christ have mercy on us!" But both thieves will not be saved, and now that the game is up, Vladimir seeks to protect himself:

> Tell him . . . (he hesitates) . . . tell him you saw me and that . . . (he hesitates) . . that you saw me [. . .] (With sudden violence.) You're sure you saw me, you won't come and tell me to-morrow that you never saw me! [p. 59a]

The "us" of the first act is the "me" of the second. Habits break, old friends are abandoned, Gogo—for the moment—is cast into the pit. When Gogo awakens, Didi is standing with his head bowed. Didi does not tell his friend of his conversation with the Boy nor of his insight or sadness. Gogo asks, "What's wrong with you," and Didi answers, "Nothing." Didi tells Estragon that they must return the following evening to keep their appointment once again. But for him the routine is meaningless: Godot will not come. There is something more than irony in his reply to Gogo's question, "And if we dropped him?" "He'd punish us," Didi says. But the punishment is already apparent to Didi: the pointless execution of orders without hope of fulfillment. Never coming; for Didi, Godot has come . . . and gone.

But Didi alone sees behind his old habits and even he, in his ironic musing, senses someone else watching him sleep just as he watches Gogo: he learns that all awareness is relative. Pozzo is no relativist, but a strict naturalist. In the first act he describes the setting of the sun with meticulous hand gestures, twice consulting his watch so as to be precise. Pozzo knows his "degrees" and the subtle shadings of time's passing. He also senses that when night comes it "will burst upon us pop! like that! just when we least expect it." And for Pozzo, once it is night there is no more time, for he measures that commodity by the sun.

Going blind, Pozzo too has an epiphany—the exact opposite of Didi's:

> *Have you not done tormenting me with your accursed time!*
> *It's abominable! When! When! One day, is that not enough*
> *for you, one day he went dumb, one day I went blind, one*
> *day we'll go deaf, one day we were born, one day we shall die,*
> *the same day, the same second, is that not enough for you?*
>
> [p. 57b]

Of the light gleaming an instant astride the grave, Pozzo has only a dim memory. He has found a new habit to accommodate his new blindness; his epiphany is false. The experience of the play indeed shows us that there is plenty of time, too much: waiting means more time than things to fill it.

Pozzo/Lucky play a special role in this passing of time that is *Waiting for Godot*'s action. Things have changed for them by Act II. Pozzo is blind and helpless, Lucky is dumb. Their "career" is nearly over. Like more conventional theatrical characters, they have passed from bad times to worse. The rope, whip, and valise remain: all else is gone—Lear and the Fool on the heath, that is what this strange pair suggests to me. But if they are that *in themselves*, they are something different to Gogo/Didi. In the first act, Gogo/Didi suspect that Pozzo may be Godot. Discovering that he is not, they are curious about him and Lucky. They circle around their new acquaintances, listen to Pozzo's speeches, taunt Lucky, and so on. Partly afraid, somewhat uncertainly, they integrate Pozzo/Lucky into their world of waiting: they make out of the visitors a way of passing time. And they exploit the *persons* of Pozzo/Lucky, taking food and playing games. (In the Free Southern Theatre production, Gogo and Didi pickpocket Pozzo, stealing his watch, pipe, and atomizer—no doubt to hock them for necessary food. This interpretation has advantages: it grounds the play in an acceptable reality; it establishes a first act relationship of double exploitation—Pozzo uses them as audience and they use him as income.) In the second act this exploitation process is even clearer. Pozzo no longer seeks an audience. Gogo/Didi no longer think that Pozzo may be Godot (Gogo, briefly, goes through this routine). Gogo/Didi try to detain Pozzo/Lucky as long as possible. They play rather cruel games with them, postponing assistance. It would be intolerable to Gogo/Didi for this "diversion" to pass quickly, just as it is intolerable for an audience to watch it go on so long. What "should" be a momentary encounter is converted into a prolonged affair. Vladimir sermonizes on their responsibilities. "It is not every day that we are needed." The talk continues without action. Then, trying to pull Pozzo up, Vladimir falls on top of him. Estragon does likewise. Obviously, they can pull Pozzo up (just as they can get up themselves). But instead they remain prone. "Won't you play with us?" they seem to be asking. But Pozzo is in no playing mood. Despite his protests, Gogo/Didi continue their game. It is, as Gogo says, "child's play." They get up, help Pozzo and Lucky up, and the play proceeds. When they are gone, Estragon goes to sleep. Vladimir shakes him awake. "I was lonely." And speaking of Pozzo/Lucky, "That passed the time." For them, perhaps; but for the audience? It is an ironic scene—the entire cast sprawled on the floor, hard to see, not much action. It makes an audience aware that the time is not passing fast enough.

This game with Pozzo/Lucky is one of many. In fact, the gamesmanship of *Waiting for Godot* is extraordinary. Most of the play is taken up by a series of word games, play acting, body games, routines. Each of these units is distinct, usually cued in by memories of *why* Gogo/Didi are where they are. Unable simply to consider the ramifications of "waiting," unfit, that is, for pure speculation (as Lucky was once fit), they fall back onto their games: how many thieves were saved, how many leaves on the tree, calling each other names, how can we hang ourselves, and so on. These games are not thematically meaningless, they feed into the rich image-texture of the play; but they are meaningless in terms of the play's action: they lead nowhere, they contribute to the non-plot. Even when Godot is discussed, the talk quickly becomes routinized. At one time

Vladimir spoke to Godot. "What exactly did we ask him for?" Estragon asks. Vladimir replies, "Were you not there?" "I can't have been listening." But it is Gogo who supplies the information that Didi confirms: That their request was "a kind of prayer . . . a vague supplication." And it is both of them, in contrapuntal chorus, who confirm that Godot would have to "think it over . . . in the quiet of his home . . . consult his family . . . his friends . . . his agents . . . his correspondents . . . his books . . . his bank account . . . before taking a decision."

This kind of conversation populates *Godot*. A discussion or argument is transformed into routinized counterpoint. Much has been said about the beauty of Beckett's prose in this play. More needs to be said about its routine qualities. Clichés are converted into game/rituals by dividing the lines between Gogo and Didi, by arbitrarily assigning one phrase to each. Thus we have a sense of their "pairdom," while we are entranced by the rhythm of their language. Beckett's genius in dialogue is his *scoring*, not his "book." This scoring pertains not only to language but to events as well. Whatever there is to do, is done in duets. By using these, Gogo/Didi are able to convert anxiety into habit. Gogo is more successful at this than Didi. For Gogo things are either forgotten at once or never forgotten. There is no "time-span" for him, only a kaleidoscopic present in which everything that is there is forever in focus. It takes Didi to remind Gogo of Godot, and these reminders always bring Gogo pain, his exasperated "Ah." For Didi the problem is more complex. Gogo says "no use wriggling" to which Didi replies, "the essential doesn't change." These are opposite contentions; that's why they harmonize so well.

A few words about Time. If waiting is the play's action, Time is its subject. Godot is not Time, but he is associated with it— the one who makes but does not keep appointments. (An impish thought occurs: Perhaps Godot passes time with Gogo/Didi just as they pass it with him. Within this scheme, Godot has nothing to do [as the Boy tells Didi in Act II] and uses the *whole play* as a diversion in his day. Thus the "big game" is a strict analogy of the many "small games" that make the play.)

The basic rhythm of the play is habit interrupted by memory, memory obliterated by games. Why do Gogo/Didi play? In order to deaden their sense of waiting. Waiting is a "waiting *for*" and it is precisely this that they wish to forget. One may say that "waiting" is the larger context within which "passing time" by playing games is a sub-system, protecting them from the sense that they are waiting. They confront Time (i.e., are conscious of Godot) only when there is a break in the games and they "know" and "feel" that they are waiting.

In conventional drama all details converge on the center of action. We may call this kind of structure centripetal. In *Godot* the action is centrifugal. Gogo/Didi do their best to shield themselves from a direct consciousness that they are at the appointed place at the prescribed time. If the center of the play is Time, dozens of activities and capers fling Gogo/Didi away from this center. But events at the periphery force them back inward: try as they will, they are not able to forget. We may illustrate the structure thus:

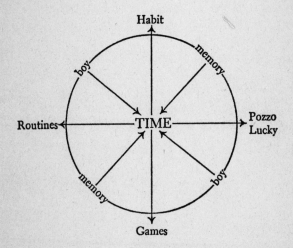

Caught on the hub of this wheel, driven by "re-minders" toward the center, Gogo/Didi literally have nowhere to go outside of this tight scheme. The scenic counterpart is the time-bracket "dusk-darkness"—that portion of the day when they must be at the appointed place. But even when night falls, and they are free to go, our last glimpse of them in each act is:

ESTRAGON: *Well, shall we go?*
VLADIMIR: *Yes, let's go.*
    They do not move.

As if to underline the duet-nature of this ending, Beckett reverses the line assignments in Act II.

What emerges is a strange solitude, again foreshadowed by Beckett in his *Proust.* "The artistic tendency is not expansive but a contraction. And art is the apotheosis of solitude." In spinning out from the center, Gogo/Didi do not go anywhere, "they do not move." Yet their best theatrical moments are all motion, a running helter-skelter, a panic. Only at the end of each act, when it is all over for the day, are they quiet. The unmoved mover is Time, that dead identicality of instant and eternity. Once each for Didi and Pozzo, everything is contracted to that sense of Time where consciousness is possible, but nothing else. To wait and not know *how* to wait is to experience Time. To be freed from waiting (as Gogo/Didi are at the end of each act) is to permit the moon to rise more rapidly than it can (as it does on *Godot*'s stage), almost as if nature were illegally celebrating its release from its own clock. Let loose from Time, night comes all of a sudden. After intermission, there is the next day—and tomorrow, another performance.

There are two time rhythms in *Godot,* one of the play and one of the stage. Theatrically, the exit of the Boy and the sudden night are strong cues for the act (and the play) to end. We, the audience, are relieved—it's almost over for us. They, the actors, do not move—even when the Godot-game is over, the theater-game keeps them in their place: tomorrow they must return to enact identical routines. Underlying the play (all of it, not just the final scene of each act) is the theater, and this is exactly what the script insinuates—a nightly appointment performed for people the characters will never meet. *Waiting for Godot* powerfully injects the mechanics of the theater into the mysteries of the play.

BIBLIOGRAPHY OF WORKS IN ENGLISH*

Books on Beckett

COE, RICHARD. *Samuel Beckett*. New York: Grove Press, Inc., 1964.

COHN, RUBY (ed.). *Modern Drama* (special issue on Beckett, December, 1966).

—— (ed.). *Perspective* (special issue on Beckett, Autumn, 1959).

——. *Samuel Beckett: The Comic Gamut*. New Brunswick, N.J.: Rutgers University Press, 1962.

DUCKWORTH, COLIN (ed.). *En attendant Godot* (a critical edition). London: George G. Harrap and Co., 1966.

ESSLIN, MARTIN (ed.). *Samuel Beckett: A Collection of Critical Essays*. Englewood Cliffs, N.J.: Prentice-Hall, 1965.

FEDERMAN, RAYMOND. *Journey to Chaos: Samuel Beckett's Early Fiction*. Berkeley, Calif.: University of California Press, 1965.

FLETCHER, JOHN. *The Novels of Samuel Beckett*. London: Chatto and Windus, 1964.

HOFFMAN, FREDERICK J. *Samuel Beckett: The Language of Self*. Carbondale, Ill.: Southern Illinois University Press, 1962.

JACOBSEN, JOSEPHINE and MUELLER, WILLIAM R. *The Testament of Samuel Beckett*. New York: Hill and Wang, 1964.

KENNER, HUGH. *Samuel Beckett: A Critical Study*. New York: Grove Press, Inc., 1961.

SCOTT, NATHAN A. *Samuel Beckett*. New York: Hillary House, 1965.

TINDALL, WILLIAM YORK. *Samuel Beckett*. New York: Columbia University Press, 1964.

Analyses of Waiting for Godot

ALLSOP, KENNETH. *The Angry Decade*. London: Peter Owen Ltd., 1958, pp. 37–42.

---

* This Bibliography was compiled from materials kindly supplied by Raymond Federman and John Fletcher.

ASHMORE, JEROME. "Philosophical Aspects of Godot," *Symposium* (Winter, 1962), pp. 296–306.

BECKETT, JEREMY. "*Waiting for Godot*," *Meanjin* (1956), pp. 216–18.

BENTLEY, ERIC. *The Life of the Drama*. New York: Atheneum, 1964, pp. 99–101, 348–51.

BLAU, HERBERT. *The Impossible Theater: A Manifesto*. New York: Macmillan, 1964, pp. 228–51.

BROUSSE, JACQUES. "Theater in Paris," *The European* (December, 1953), pp. 39–43.

BUTLER, HARRY L. "Balzac and Godeau, Beckett and Godot: A Curious Parallel," *Romance Notes* (Spring, 1962), pp. 13–17.

CHADWICK, C. "*Waiting for Godot*: A Logical Approach," *Symposium* (Winter, 1960), pp. 252–57.

CHAUCER, DANIEL. "*Waiting for Godot*," *Shenandoah* (Spring, 1955), pp. 80–82.

CHIARI, JOSEPH. *Landmarks of Contemporary Drama*. London: Herbert Jenkins, 1965, pp. 68–80.

CLURMAN, HAROLD. *Lies Like Truth*. New York: Macmillan, 1958, pp. 220–22.

COHEN, ROBERT S. "Parallels and the Possibility of Influence Between Simone Weil's *Waiting for God* and Samuel Beckett's *Waiting for Godot*." *Modern Drama* (February, 1964), pp. 425–36.

COHN, RUBY. "The Absurdly Absurd: Avatars of *Godot*," *Comparative Literature Studies*, II, 3 (1965), 233–40.

———. "Waiting Is All," *Modern Drama* (September, 1960), pp. 162–67.

COLE, CONNELLY. "A Note on *Waiting for Godot*," *Icarus* (January, 1957), pp. 25–27.

DUKORE, BERNARD. "Gogo, Didi, and the Absent Godot," *Drama Survey* (Winter, 1962), pp. 301–307.

ESSLIN, MARTIN. "Godot and His Children" in William A. Armstrong, ed., *Experimental Drama* (London: G. Bell & Sons, 1963), pp. 128–46.

———. *The Theatre of the Absurd*. New York: Doubleday and Co., 1961, pp. 13–27.

FLETCHER, JOHN. "Beckett and Balzac Revisited," *French Review* (October, 1963), pp. 78–80.

FLOOD, ETHELBERT. "A Reading of Beckett's *Godot*," *Culture* (September, 1961), pp. 257–62.

FOWLIE, WALLACE. *Dionysus in Paris*. New York: Meridian Books, 1960, pp. 210–17.

FRANCIS, RICHARD LEE. "Beckett's Metaphysical Tragicomedy," *Modern Drama* (December, 1965), pp. 259–67.

GASSNER, JOHN. *Theatre at the Crossroads*. New York: Holt, Rinehart & Winston, 1960, pp. 252–56.

GLICKSBERG, CHARLES. *The Self in Modern Literature*. University Park, Pennsylvania: Pennsylvania State University Press, 1963, pp. 117–21.

GOLD, HERBERT. "Beckett: Style and Desire," *Nation* (November 10, 1956), pp. 397–99.

GRAY, RONALD. "*Waiting for Godot*: A Christian Interpretation," *Listener* (January 24, 1957), pp. 160–61.

GROSSVOGEL, DAVID. *The Self-Conscious Stage in Modern French Drama*. New York: Columbia University Press, 1958, pp. 324–34.

———. *Four Playwrights and a Postscript: Brecht, Ionesco, Beckett, Genet*. Ithaca, N.Y.: Cornell University Press, 1962, pp. 86–109.

GUICHARNAUD, JACQUES. *Modern French Theater from Giraudoux to Beckett*. New Haven: Yale University Press, 1961, pp. 193–216.

HOBSON, HAROLD. "Samuel Beckett, Dramatist of the Year," in *International Theatre Annual*, No. 1 (London: John Calder, 1956), pp. 153–55.

HOOKER, WARD. "Irony and Absurdity in the Avant-Garde Theater," *Kenyon Review* (Summer, 1960), pp. 436–54.

HUGHES, CATHERINE. "Beckett and the Game of Life," *The Catholic World* (June, 1962), pp. 163–68.

KERN, EDITH. "Drama Stripped for Inaction: Beckett's *Godot*," *Yale French Studies* (Winter, 1954–1955), pp. 41–47.

KILLINGER, JOHN. *The Failure of Theology in Modern Literature*. New York: Abingdon Press, 1963, pp. 215–17.

LEE, WARREN. "The Bitter Pill of Samuel Beckett," *Chicago Review* (Winter, 1957), pp. 77–87.

LEVENTHAL, A. J. "Mr. Beckett's *En attendant Godot*," *Dublin Magazine* (April–June, 1954), pp. 11–16.

LEWIS, ALLAN. *The Contemporary Theater: The Significant Playwrights of Our Time*. New York: Crown, 1962, pp. 259–81.

MacNeice, Louis. *Varieties of Parable.* London: Cambridge University Press, 1965, pp. 119–29, 140–43.

Marinello, Leone J. "Samuel Beckett's *Waiting for Godot,*" *Drama Critique* (Spring, 1963), pp. 75–81.

Markus, Thomas B. "Bernard Dukore and *Waiting for Godot,*" *Drama Survey* (February, 1963), pp. 360–63.

McCoy, Charles. "*Waiting for Godot:* A Biblical Approach," *Florida Review* (Spring, 1958), pp. 63–72.

Mercier, Vivian. "A Pyrrhonian Eclogue," *The Hudson Review,* Vol. VII, No. 4 (Winter, 1955), pp. 620–24.

Moore, John R. "A Farewell to Something," *Tulane Drama Review* (September, 1960), pp. 49–60.

Politzer, Heinz. "The Egghead Waits for Godot," *Christian Scholar* (March, 1959), pp. 46–50.

Pronko, Leonard C. "Beckett, Ionesco, Schéhadé: The Avant-Garde Theatre," *Modern Language Forum* (December, 1958), pp. 118–23.

———. *Avant-Garde: The Experimental Theater in France.* Berkeley, California: University of California Press, 1962, pp. 25–39.

Radke, Judith. "The Theatre of Samuel Beckett: Une durée à animer," *Yale French Studies* (Spring–Summer, 1962), pp. 57–64.

Reid, Alec. "Beckett and the Drama of Unknowing," *Drama Survey* (October, 1962), pp. 130–38.

Rechtien, Brother John, S.M. "Time and Eternity Meet in the Present," *Texas Studies in Language and Literature* (Spring, 1964), pp. 5–21.

Rexroth, Kenneth. "The Point Is Irrelevance," *The Nation* (April 14, 1956), pp. 325–28.

Rhodes, S. A. "From Godeau to Godot," *French Review* (January, 1963), pp. 260–65.

Schneider, Pierre. "Play and Display," *The Listener* (January 28, 1954), pp. 174–76.

Simpson, Alan. *Beckett and Behan, and a Theatre in Dublin.* London: Routledge & Kegan Paul, 1962, pp. 62–97, 98–137.

de Stefano, Sister Mary Venise, W.S. "Man's Search for Meaning in Modern French Drama," *Renascence* (Winter, 1964), pp. 81–91.

Styan, J. L. *The Dark Comedy.* Cambridge: The University Press, 1962, pp. 227–29.

TALLMER, JERRY. "Godot on Broadway" and "Godot: Still Waiting" in Daniel Wolf and Edwin Fancher, eds. *Village Voice Reader*. New York: Doubleday, 1962. Reprinted by Grove Press, 1963, pp. 60–66.

TYNAN, KENNETH. *Tynan on Theatre*. New York: Atheneum, 1961, pp. 36–38.

VAHANIAN, GABRIEL. "The Empty Cradle," *Theology Today* (January 4, 1957), pp. 521–26.

VIA, D. O. JR. "*Waiting for Godot* and Man's Search for Community," *Journal of Bible and Religion* (January, 1962), pp. 32–37.

WELLWARTH, GEORGE E. *The Theater of Protest and Paradox*. New York: New York University Press, 1964, pp. 37–51.

WHITTICK, ARNOLD. *Symbols, Signs and Their Meaning*. London: Leonard Hill, 1960, pp. 372–74.

WILLIAMS, RAYMOND. *Modern Tragedy*. London: Chatto & Windus, 1966, pp. 153–55.

WORSLEY, T. C. "Cactus Land," *New Statesman and Nation* (August 13, 1955), pp. 184–85.